Pittsburgh Pirates 2021

A Baseball Companion

Edited by Steven Goldman and Bret Sayre

Baseball Prospectus

Craig Brown, Associate Editor
Robert Au, Harry Pavlidis and Amy Pircher, Statistics Editors

Library of Congress Cataloging-in-Publication Data:
paperback
ISBN-13: 978-1-950716-67-8

Project Credits
Cover Design: Ginny Searle
Interior Design and Production: Amy Pircher, Robert Au
Layout: Amy Pircher, Robert Au

Baseball icon courtesy of Uberux, from https://www.shareicon.net/author/uberux

Ballpark diagram courtesy of Lou Spirito/THIRTY81 Project, https://thirty81project.com/

Manufactured in the United States of America
10 9 8 7 6 5 4 3 2 1

Table of Contents

Statistical Introduction v

Part 1: Team Analysis

Performance Graphs 3

2020 Team Performance 4

2021 Team Projections 5

Team Personnel 6

PNC Park Stats 7

Pirates Team Analysis 9

Part 2: Player Analysis

Pirates Player Analysis 16

Pirates Prospects 91

Part 3: Featured Articles

Pirates All-Time Top 10 Players 103
  by Matthew Trueblood

A Taxonomy of 2020 Abnormalities 109
  by Rob Mains

Tranches of WAR 115
  by Russell A. Carleton

Secondhand Sport 121
  by Patrick Dubuque

Steve Dalkowski Dreaming 125
  by Steven Goldman

A Reward For A Functioning Society 129
  by Cory Frontin and Craig Goldstein

Index of Names 133

Statistical Introduction

Sports are, fundamentally, a blend of athletic endeavor and storytelling. Baseball, like any other sport, tells its stories in so many ways: in the arc of a game from the stands or a season from the box scores, in photos, or even in numbers. At Baseball Prospectus, we understand that statistics don't replace observation or any of baseball's stories, but complement everything else that makes the game so much fun.

What stats help us with is with patterns and precision, variance and value. This book can help you learn things you may not see from watching a game or hundred, whether it's the path of a career over time or the breadth of the entire MLB. We'd also never ask you to choose between our numbers and the experience of viewing a game from the cheap seats or the comfort of your home; our publication combines running the numbers with observations and wisdom from some of the brightest minds we can find. But if you *do* want to learn more about the numbers beyond what's on the backs of player jerseys, let us help explain.

Offense

We've revised our methodology for determining batting value. Long-time readers of the book will notice that we've retired True Average in favor of a new metric: Deserved Runs Created Plus (DRC+). Developed by Jonathan Judge and our stats team, this statistic measures everything a player does at the plate–reaching base, hitting for power, making outs, and moving runners over–and puts it on a scale where 100 equals league-average performance. A DRC+ of 150 is terrific, a DRC+ of 100 is average and a DRC+ of 75 means you better be an excellent defender.

DRC+ also does a better job than any of our previous metrics in taking contextual factors into account. The model adjusts for how the park affects performance, but also for things like the talent of the opposing pitcher, value of different types of batted-ball events, league, temperature and other factors. It's able to describe a player's expected offensive contribution than any other statistic we've found over the years, and also does a better job of predicting future performance as well.

The other aspect of run-scoring is baserunning, which we quantify using Baserunning Runs. BRR not only records the value of stolen bases (or getting caught in the act), but also accounts for all the stuff that doesn't show up on the back of a baseball card: a runner's ability to go first to third on a single, or advance on a fly ball.

Defense

Where offensive value is *relatively* easy to identify and understand, defensive value is ... not. Over the past dozen years, the sabermetric community has focused mostly on stats based on zone data: a real-live human person records the type of batted ball and estimated landing location, and models are created that give expected outs. From there, you can compare fielders' actual outs to those expected ones. Simple, right?

Unfortunately, zone data has two major issues. First, zone data is recorded by commercial data providers who keep the raw data private unless you pay for it. (All the statistics we build in this book and on our website use public data as inputs.) That hurts our ability to test assumptions or duplicate results. Second, over the years it has become apparent that there's quite a bit of "noise" in zone-based fielding analysis. Sometimes the conclusions drawn from zone data don't hold up to scrutiny, and sometimes the different data provided by different providers don't look anything alike, giving wildly different results. Sometimes the hard-working professional stringers or scorers might unknowingly inflict unconscious bias into the mix: for example good fielders will often be credited with more expected outs despite the data, and ballparks with high press boxes tend to score more line drives than ones with a lower press box.

Enter our Fielding Runs Above Average (FRAA). For most positions, FRAA is built from play-by-play data, which allows us to avoid the subjectivity found in many other fielding metrics. The idea is this: count how many fielding plays are made by a given player and compare that to expected plays for an average fielder at their position (based on pitcher ground ball tendencies and batter handedness). Then we adjust for park and base-out situations.

When it comes to catchers, our methodology is a little different thanks to the laundry list of responsibilities they're tasked with beyond just, well, catching and throwing the ball. By now you've probably heard about "framing" or the art of making umpires more likely to call balls outside the strike zone for strikes. To put this into one tidy number, we incorporate pitch tracking data (for the years it exists) and adjust for important factors like pitcher, umpire, batter and home-field advantage using a mixed-model approach. This grants us a number for how many strikes the catcher is personally adding to (or subtracting from) his pitchers' performance ... which we then convert to runs added or lost using linear weights.

Framing is one of the biggest parts of determining catcher value, but we also take into account blocking balls from going past, whether a scorer deems it a passed ball or a wild pitch. We use a similar approach—one that really benefits from the pitch tracking data that tells us what ends up in the dirt and what doesn't. We also include a catcher's ability to prevent stolen bases and how well they field balls in play, and *finally* we come up with our FRAA for catchers.

Pitching

Both pitching and fielding make up the half of baseball that isn't run scoring: run prevention. Separating pitching from fielding is a tough task, and most recent pitching analysis has branched off from Voros McCracken's famous (and controversial) statement, "There is little if any difference among major-league pitchers in their ability to prevent hits on balls hit in the field of play." The research of the analytic community has validated this to some extent, and there are a host of "defense-independent" pitching measures that have been developed to try and extract the effect of the defense behind a hurler from the pitcher's work.

Our solution to this quandary is Deserved Run Average (DRA), our core pitching metric. DRA seeks to evaluate a pitcher's performance, much like earned run average (ERA), the tried-and-true pitching stat you've seen on every baseball broadcast or box score from the past century, but it's very different. To start, DRA takes an event-by-event look at what the pitchers does, and adjusts the value of that event based on different environmental factors like park, batter, catcher, umpire, base-out situation, run differential, inning, defense, home field advantage, pitcher role and temperature. That mixed model gives us a pitcher's expected contribution, similar to what we do for our DRC+ model for hitters and FRAA model for catchers. (Oh, and we also consider the pitcher's effect on basestealing and on balls getting past the catcher.)

DRA is set to the scale of runs allowed per nine innings (RA9) instead of ERA, which makes DRA's scale slightly higher than ERA's. Because of this, for ease of use, we're supplying DRA-, which is much easier for the reader to parse. As with DRC+, DRA- is an "index" stat, meaning instead of using some arbitrary and shifting number to denote what's "good," average is always 100. The reason that it uses a minus rather than a plus is because like ERA, a lower number is better. Therefore a 75 DRA- describes a performance 25 percent better than average, whereas a 150 DRA- means that either a pitcher is getting extremely lucky with their results, or getting ready to try a new pitch.

Since the last time you picked up an edition of this book, we've also made a few minor changes to DRA to make it better. Recent research into "tunneling"—the act of throwing consecutive pitches that appear similar from a batter's point of view until after the swing decision point–data has given us a new contextual factor to account for in DRA: plate distance. This refers to the distance between successive pitches as they approach the plate, and while it has a smaller effect than factors like velocity or whiff rate, it still can help explain pitcher strikeout rate in our model.

Recently Added Descriptive Statistics

Returning to our 2021 edition of the book are a few figures which recently appeared. These numbers may be a little bit more familiar to those of you who have spent some time investigating baseball statistics.

Fastball Percentage

Our fastball percentage (FA%) statistic measures how frequently a pitcher throws a pitch classified as a "fastball," measured as a percentage of overall pitches thrown. We qualify three types of fastballs:

1. The traditional four-seam fastball;
2. The two-seam fastball or sinker;
3. "Hard cutters," which are pitches that have the movement profile of a cut fastball and are used as the pitcher's primary offering or in place of a more traditional fastball.

For example, a pitcher with a FA% of 67 throws any combination of these three pitches about two-thirds of the time.

Whiff Rate

Everybody loves a swing and a miss, and whiff rate (Whiff%) measures how frequently pitchers induce a swinging strike. To calculate Whiff%, we add up all the pitches thrown that ended with a swinging strike, then divide that number by a pitcher's total pitches thrown. Most often, high whiff rates correlate with high strikeout rates (and overall effective pitcher performance).

Called Strike Probability

Called Strike Probability (CSP) is a number that represents the likelihood that all of a pitcher's pitches will be called a strike while controlling for location, pitcher and batter handedness, umpire and count. Here's how it works: on each pitch, our model determines how many times (out of 100) that a similar pitch was called for a strike given those factors mentioned above, and when normalized for each batter's strike zone. Then we average the CSP for all pitches thrown by a pitcher in a season, and that gives us the yearly CSP percentage you see in the stats boxes.

As you might imagine, pitchers with a higher CSP are more likely to work in the zone, where pitchers with a lower CSP are likely locating their pitches outside the normal strike zone, for better or for worse.

Projections

Many of you aren't turning to this book just for a look at what a player has done, but for a look at what a player is going to do: the PECOTA projections. PECOTA, initially developed by Nate Silver (who has moved on to greater fame as a political analyst), consists of three parts:

1. Major-league equivalencies, which use minor-league statistics to project how a player will perform in the major leagues;
2. Baseline forecasts, which use weighted averages and regression to the mean to estimate a player's current true talent level; and
3. Aging curves, which uses the career paths of comparable players to estimate how a player's statistics are likely to change over time.

With all those important things covered, let's take a look at what's in the book this year.

Team Prospectus

Most of this book is composed of team chapters, with one for each of the 30 major-league franchises. On the first page of each chapter, you'll see a box that contains some of the key statistics for each team as well as a very inviting stadium diagram.

We start with the team name, their unadjusted 2020 win-loss record, and their divisional ranking. Beneath that are a host of other team statistics. **Pythag** presents an adjusted 2020 winning percentage, calculated by taking runs scored per game (**RS/G**) and runs allowed per game (**RA/G**) for the team, and running them through a version of Bill James' Pythagorean formula that was refined and improved by David Smyth and Brandon Heipp. (The formula is called "Pythagenpat," which is equally fun to type and to say.)

Next up is **DRC+**, described earlier, to indicate the overall hitting ability of the team either above or below league-average. Run prevention on the pitching side is covered by **DRA** (also mentioned earlier) and another metric: Fielding Independent Pitching (**FIP**), which calculates another ERA-like statistic based on strikeouts, walks, and home runs recorded. Defensive Efficiency Rating (**DER**) tells us the percentage of balls in play turned into outs for the team, and is a quick fielding shorthand that rounds out run prevention.

After that, we have several measures related to roster composition, as opposed to on-field performance. **B-Age** and **P-Age** tell us the average age of a team's batters and pitchers, respectively. **Payroll** is the combined team payroll for all on-field players, and Doug Pappas' Marginal Dollars per Marginal Win (**M$/MW**) tells us how much money a team spent to earn production above replacement level.

Next to each of these stats, we've listed each team's MLB rank in that category from first to 30th. In this, first always indicates a positive outcome and 30th a negative outcome, except in the case of salary—first is highest.

After the franchise statistics, we share a few items about the team's home ballpark. There's the aforementioned diagram of the park's dimensions (including distances to the outfield wall), a graphic showing the height of the wall from the left-field pole to the right-field pole, and a table showing three-year park factors for the stadium. The park factors are displayed as indexes where 100 is average, 110 means that the park inflates the statistic in question by 10 percent, and 90 means that the park deflates the statistic in question by 10 percent.

On the second page of each team chapter, you'll find three graphs. The first is **Payroll History** and helps you see how the team's payroll has compared to the MLB and divisional average payrolls over time. Payroll figures are current as of January 1, 2021; with so many free agents still unsigned as of this writing, the final 2021 figure will likely be significantly different for many teams. (In the meantime, you can always find the most current data at Baseball Prospectus' Cot's Baseball Contracts page.)

The second graph is **Future Commitments** and helps you see the team's future outlays, if any.

The third graph is **Farm System Ranking** and displays how the Baseball Prospectus prospect team has ranked the organization's farm system since 2007.

After the graphs, we have a **Personnel** section that lists many of the important decision-makers and upper-level field and operations staff members for the franchise, as well as any former Baseball Prospectus staff members who are currently part of the organization. (In very rare circumstances, someone might be on both lists!)

Position Players

After all that information and a thoughtful bylined essay covering each team, we present our player comments. These are also bylined, but due to frequent franchise shifts during the offseason, our bylines are more a rough guide than a perfect accounting of who wrote what.

Each player is listed with the major-league team that employed him as of early January 2021. If a player changed teams after that point via free agency, trade, or any other method, you'll be able to find them in the chapter for their previous squad.

As an example, take a look at the player comment for Padres shortstop Fernando Tatis Jr.: the stat block that accompanies his written comment is at the top of this page. First we cover biographical information (age is as of June 30, 2021) before moving onto the stats themselves. Our statistic columns include standard identifying information like **YEAR**, **TEAM**, **LVL** (level of affiliated play) and **AGE** before getting into the numbers. Next, we provide raw, untranslated

Fernando Tatis Jr. SS

Born: 01/02/99   Age: 22   Bats: R   Throws: R
Height: 6'3"   Weight: 217   Origin: International Free Agent, 2015

YEAR	TEAM	LVL	AGE	PA	R	2B	3B	HR	RBI	BB	K	SB	CS	AVG/OBP/SLG
2018	SA	AA	19	394	77	22	4	16	43	33	109	16	5	.286/.355/.507
2019	SD	MLB	20	372	61	13	6	22	53	30	110	16	6	.317/.379/.590
2020	SD	MLB	21	257	50	11	2	17	45	27	61	11	3	.277/.366/.571
2021 FS	SD	MLB	22	600	95	24	4	31	81	50	165	17	8	.263/.331/.499
2021 DC	SD	MLB	22	628	100	25	4	32	85	53	173	19	8	.263/.331/.499

Comparables: Darryl Strawberry, Bo Bichette, Ronald Acuña Jr.

YEAR	TEAM	LVL	AGE	PA	DRC+	BABIP	BRR	FRAA	WARP
2018	SA	AA	19	394	136	.370	3.0	SS(83): -1.9	2.4
2019	SD	MLB	20	372	118	.410	7.1	SS(83): 0.9	3.4
2020	SD	MLB	21	257	126	.306	0.7	SS(57): -5.5	0.9
2021 FS	SD	MLB	22	600	126	.318	1.7	SS -1	3.9
2021 DC	SD	MLB	22	628	126	.318	1.8	SS -1	4.0

numbers like you might find on the back of your dad's baseball cards: **PA** (plate appearances), **R** (runs), **2B** (doubles), **3B** (triples), **HR** (home runs), **RBI** (runs batted in), **BB** (walks), **K** (strikeouts), **SB** (stolen bases) and **CS** (caught stealing).

Following the basic stats is **Whiff%** (whiff rate), which denotes how often, when a batter swings, he fails to make contact with the ball. Another way to think of this number is an inverse of a hitter's contact rate.

Next, we have unadjusted "slash" statistics: **AVG** (batting average), **OBP** (on-base percentage) and **SLG** (slugging percentage). Following the slash line is **DRC+** (Deserved Runs Created Plus), which we described earlier as total offensive expected contribution compared to the league average.

BABIP (batting average on balls in play) tells us how often a ball in play fell for a hit, and can help us identify whether a batter may have been lucky or not ... but note that high BABIPs also tend to follow the great hitters of our time, as well as speedy singles hitters who put the ball on the ground.

The next item is **BRR** (Baserunning Runs), which covers all of a player's baserunning accomplishments including (but not limited to) swiped bags and failed attempts. Next is **FRAA** (Fielding Runs Above Average), which also includes the number of games previously played at each position noted in parentheses. Multi-position players have only their two most frequent positions listed here, but their total FRAA number reflects all positions played.

Our last column here is **WARP** (Wins Above Replacement Player). WARP estimates the total value of a player, which means for hitters it takes into account hitting runs above average (calculated using the DRC+ model), BRR and FRAA. Then, it makes an adjustment for positions played and gives the player a credit for plate appearances based upon the difference between "replacement level"—which is derived from the quality of players added to a team's roster after the start of the season–and the league average.

The final line just below the stats box is **PECOTA** data, which is discussed further in a following section.

Catchers

Catchers are a special breed, and thus they have earned their own separate box which displays some of the defensive metrics that we've built just for them. As an example, let's check out Yasmani Grandal.

YEAR	TEAM	P. COUNT	FRM RUNS	BLK RUNS	THRW RUNS	TOT RUNS
2018	LAD	16816	15.7	0.8	0.1	16.5
2019	MIL	18740	19.4	1.8	-0.1	21.1
2020	CHW	4830	3.7	0.3	-0.2	3.8
2021	CHW	14430	16.7	-0.6	1.0	17.1
2021	CHW	14430	16.7	0.4	1.0	18.0

The **YEAR** and **TEAM** columns match what you'd find in the other stat box. **P. COUNT** indicates the number of pitches thrown while the catcher was behind the plate, including swinging strikes, fouls and balls in play. **FRM RUNS** is the total run value the catcher provided (or cost) his team by influencing the umpire to call strikes where other catchers did not. **BLK RUNS** expresses the total run value above or below average for the catcher's ability to prevent wild pitches and passed balls. **THRW RUNS** is calculated using a similar model as the previous two statistics, and it measures a catcher's ability to throw out basestealers but also to dissuade them from testing his arm in the first place. It takes into account factors like the pitcher (including his delivery and pickoff move) and baserunner (who could be as fast as Billy Hamilton or as slow as Yonder Alonso). **TOT RUNS** is the sum of all of the previous three statistics.

Pitchers

Let's give our pitchers a turn, using 2020 AL Cy Young winner Shane Bieber as our example. Take a look at his stat block: the first line and the **YEAR, TEAM, LVL** and **AGE** columns are the same as in the position player example earlier.

Here too, we have a series of columns that display raw, unadjusted statistics compiled by the pitcher over the course of a season: **W** (wins), **L** (losses), **SV** (saves), **G** (games pitched), **GS** (games started), **IP** (innings pitched), **H** (hits allowed) and **HR** (home runs allowed). Next we have two statistics that are rates: **BB/9** (walks per nine innings) and **K/9** (strikeouts per nine innings), before returning to the unadjusted K (strikeouts).

ᴺext up is **GB%** (ground ball percentage), which is the percentage of all batted balls that were hit on the ground, including both outs and hits. Remember, this is based on observational data and subject to human error, so please approach this with a healthy dose of skepticism.

BABIP (batting average on balls in play) is calculated using the same methodology as it is for position players, but it often tells us more about a pitcher than it does a hitter. With pitchers, a high BABIP is often due to poor defense or bad luck, and can often be an indicator of potential rebound, and a low BABIP may be cause to expect performance regression. (A typical league-average BABIP is close to .290-.300.)

The metrics **WHIP** (walks plus hits per inning pitched) and **ERA** (earned run average) are old standbys: WHIP measures walks and hits allowed on a per-inning basis, while ERA measures earned runs on a nine-inning basis. Neither of these stats are translated or adjusted.

DRA- (Deserved Run Average) was described at length earlier, and measures how the pitcher "deserved" to perform compared to other pitchers. Please note that since we lack all the data points that would make for a "real" DRA for minor-league events, the DRA- displayed for minor league partial-seasons is based off of different data. (That data is a modified version of our cFIP metric, which you can find more information about on our website.)

Shane Bieber RHP

Born: 05/31/95   Age: 26   Bats: R   Throws: R
Height: 6'3"   Weight: 200   Origin: Round 4, 2016 Draft (#122 overall)

YEAR	TEAM	LVL	AGE	W	L	SV	G	GS	IP	H	HR	BB/9	K/9	K	GB%	BABIP
2018	AKR	AA	23	3	0	0	5	5	31	26	1	0.3	8.7	30	47.3%	.278
2018	COL	AAA	23	3	1	0	8	8	48^2	30	3	1.1	8.7	47	52.0%	.227
2018	CLE	MLB	23	11	5	0	20	19	114^2	130	13	1.8	9.3	118	46.2%	.356
2019	CLE	MLB	24	15	8	0	34	33	214^1	186	31	1.7	10.9	259	44.4%	.298
2020	CLE	MLB	25	8	1	0	12	12	77^1	46	7	2.4	14.2	122	48.4%	.267
2021 FS	CLE	MLB	26	10	6	0	26	26	150	121	18	2.1	11.7	195	45.5%	.297
2021 DC	CLE	MLB	26	14	7	0	30	30	196.7	159	24	2.1	11.7	257	45.5%	.297

Comparables: Luis Severino, Danny Salazar, Joe Musgrove

YEAR	TEAM	LVL	AGE	WHIP	ERA	DRA-	WARP	MPH	FB%	WHF	CSP
2018	AKR	AA	23	0.87	1.16	61	0.9				
2018	COL	AAA	23	0.74	1.66	69	1.2				
2018	CLE	MLB	23	1.33	4.55	74	2.6	94.7	57.4%	26.2%	
2019	CLE	MLB	24	1.05	3.28	75	4.9	94.4	45.8%	30.8%	
2020	CLE	MLB	25	0.87	1.63	53	2.6	95.3	53.6%	40.7%	
2021 FS	CLE	MLB	26	1.04	2.44	64	4.4	94.7	50.0%	33.2%	44.2%
2021 DC	CLE	MLB	26	1.04	2.44	64	5.8	94.7	50.0%	33.2%	44.2%

Just like with hitters, **WARP** (Wins Above Replacement Player) is a total value metric that puts pitchers of all stripes on the same scale as position players. We use DRA as the primary input for our calculation of WARP. You might notice that relief pitchers (due to their limited innings) may have a lower WARP than you were expecting or than you might see in other WARP-like metrics. WARP does not take leverage into account, just the actions a pitcher performs and the expected value of those actions ... which ends up judging high-leverage relief pitchers differently than you might imagine given their prestige and market value.

MPH gives you the pitcher's 95th percentile velocity for the noted season, in order to give you an idea of what the *peak* fastball velocity a pitcher possesses. Since this comes from our pitch-tracking data, it is not publicly available for minor-league pitchers.

Finally, we display the three new pitching metrics we described earlier. **FB%** (fastball percentage) gives you the percentage of fastballs thrown out of all pitches. **WHF** (whiff rate) tells you the percentage of swinging strikes induced out of all pitches. **CSP** (called strike probability) expresses the likelihood of all pitches thrown to result in a called strike, after controlling for factors like handedness, umpire, pitch type, count and location.

PECOTA

All players have PECOTA projections for 2021, as well as a set of other numbers that describe the performance of comparable players according to PECOTA. All projections for 2021 are for the player at the date we went to press in early January and are projected into the league and park context as indicated by the team abbreviation. (Note that players at very low levels of the minors are too unpredictable to assess using these numbers.) All PECOTA projected statistics represent a player's projected major-league performance.

How we're doing that is a little different this season. There are really two different values that go into the final stat line that you see for PECOTA: How a player performs, and how much playing time he'll be given to perform it. In the past we've estimated playing time based on each team's roster and depth charts, and we'll continue to do that. These projections are denoted as **2021 DC**.

But in many cases, a player won't be projected for major-league playing time; most of the time this is because they aren't projected to be major-league players at all, but still developing as prospects. Or perhaps a player will provide Triple-A depth, only to have an opportunity open up because of injury. For these purposes, we're also supplying a second projection, labeled **2021 FS**, or full season. This is what we would project the player to provide in 600 plate appearances or 150 innings pitched.

Below the projections are the player's three highest-scoring comparable players as determined by PECOTA. All comparables represent a snapshot of how the listed player was performing at the same age as the current player, so if a

23-year-old pitcher is compared to Bartolo Colón, he's actually being compared to a 23-year-old Colón, not the version that pitched for the Rangers in 2018, nor to Colón's career as a whole.

A few points about pitcher projections. First, we aren't yet projecting peak velocity, so that column will be blank in the PECOTA lines. Second, projecting DRA is trickier than evaluating past performance, because it is unclear how deserving each pitcher will be of his anticipated outcomes. However, we know that another DRA-related statistic–contextual FIP or cFIP-estimates future run scoring very well. So for PECOTA, the projected DRA- figures you see are based on the past cFIPs generated by the pitcher and comparable players over time, along with the other factors described above.

If you're familiar with PECOTA, then you'll have noticed that the projection system often appears bullish on players coming off a bad year and bearish on players coming off a good year. (This is because the system weights several previous seasons, not just the most recent one.) In addition, we publish the 50th percentile projections for each player–which is smack in the middle of the range of projected production—which tends to mean PECOTA stat lines don't often have extreme results like 40 home runs or 250 strikeouts in a given season. In essence, PECOTA doesn't project very many extreme seasons.

Managers

After all those wonderful team chapters, we've got statistics for each big-league manager, all of whom are organized by alphabetical order. Here you'll find a block including an extraordinary amount of information collected from each manager's entire career. For more information on the acronyms and what they mean, please visit the Glossary at www.baseballprospectus.com.

There is one important metric that we'd like to call attention to, and you'll find it next to each manager's name: **wRM+** (weighted reliever management plus). Developed by Rob Arthur and Rian Watt, wRM+ investigates how good a manager is at using their best relievers during the moments of highest leverage, using both our proprietary DRA metric as well as Leverage Index. wRM+ is scaled to a league average of 100, and a wRM+ of 105 indicates that relievers were used approximately five percent "better" than average. On the other hand, a wRM+ of 95 would tell us the team used its relievers five percent "worse" than the average team.

While wRM+ does not have an extremely strong correlation with a manager, it is statistically significant; this means that a manager is not *entirely* responsible for a team's wRM+, but does have some effect on that number.

Part 1: Team Analysis

Performance Graphs

Payroll History (in millions)

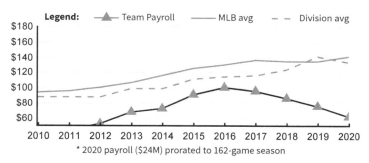

* 2020 payroll ($24M) prorated to 162-game season

Future Commitments (in millions)

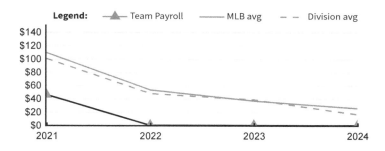

Farm System Ranking

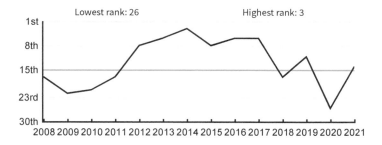

2020 Team Performance

ACTUAL STANDINGS

Team	W	L	Pct
CHC	34	26	0.567
CIN	31	29	0.517
STL	30	28	0.517
MIL	29	31	0.483
PIT	19	41	0.317

dWIN% STANDINGS

Team	W	L	Pct
CIN	32	28	0.537
MIL	29	31	0.496
CHC	27	33	0.465
STL	26	34	0.436
PIT	20	40	0.344

TOP HITTERS

Player	WARP
Adam Frazier	1.0
Jacob Stallings	0.8
Ke'Bryan Hayes	0.7

TOP PITCHERS

Player	WARP
Joe Musgrove	0.9
JT Brubaker	0.8
Chris Stratton	0.6

VITAL STATISTICS

Statistic Name	Value	Rank
Pythagenpat	.361	29th
dWin%	.344	28th
Runs Scored per Game	3.65	30th
Runs Allowed per Game	4.97	19th
Deserved Runs Created Plus	85	29th
Deserved Run Average Minus	108	23rd
Fielding Independent Pitching	4.86	21st
Defensive Efficiency Rating	.706	10th
Batter Age	27.8	4th
Pitcher Age	28.2	13th
Payroll	$24.0M	30th
Marginal $ per Marginal Win	$6.3M	25th

2021 Team Projections

PROJECTED STANDINGS

Team	W	L	Pct	+/-
MIL	89.1	72.9	0.550	10
Adding Kolten Wong doesn't quite make this an above-average lineup, but it improves their run prevention. Playoff hopes hinge on Christian Yelich being himself again.				
CHC	84.9	77.1	0.524	-6
Change, though painful, will give them an overdue chance to evaluate new options.				
STL	80.4	81.6	0.496	0
Nolan Arenado makes them favorites in the NL Central, but real parity with the goliaths on the coasts is still a ways off.				
CIN	79.3	82.7	0.490	-4
Traded or non-tendered several key role players to save money, and their Cy Young winner left as a free agent.				
PIT	**59.5**	**102.5**	**0.367**	**8**
This year will be about sorting out shortstop, hoping for progress from Mitch Keller, and enjoying Ke'Bryan Hayes--but not much more.				

TOP PROJECTED HITTERS

Player	WARP
Bryan Reynolds	2.1
Adam Frazier	2.0
Ke'Bryan Hayes	1.6

TOP PROJECTED PITCHERS

Player	WARP
Mitch Keller	1.3
Richard Rodríguez	1.1
Tyler Anderson	1.1

FARM SYSTEM REPORT

Top Prospect	Number of Top 101 Prospects
Ke'Bryan Hayes, #7	2

KEY DEDUCTIONS

Player	WARP
Joe Musgrove	2.5
Jameson Taillon	1.9
Josh Bell	1.6
Chris Archer	1.4
Trevor Williams	1.1

KEY ADDITIONS

Player	WARP
David Bednar	0.3
Sean Poppen	0.3

Team Personnel

President
Travis Williams

General Manager
Ben Cherington

Assistant General Manager
Kevan Graves

Assistant General Manager
Steve Sanders

Senior Vice President, Baseball Development
Bryan Stroh

Manager
Derek Shelton

BP Alumni
Dan Fox
Grant Jones

PNC Park Stats

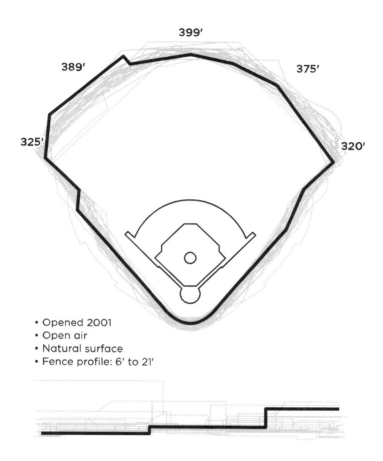

399'

389'

375'

325'

320'

- Opened 2001
- Open air
- Natural surface
- Fence profile: 6' to 21'

Three-Year Park Factors

Runs	Runs/RH	Runs/LH	HR/RH	HR/LH
96	96	96	89	98

Pirates Team Analysis

*C*ueeeeeeetoooooo. Cueeeeeeetoooooo.

The Pirates will not win a World Series in my lifetime, for reasons that are already apparent or will become apparent. But that doesn't bother me much, because 2013 gave me a better night than any championship ever could. Unintentionally, the Pittsburgh Baseball Club created that moment with two decades of consistent ineptitude.

It was the 2013 National League Wild Card Game. Bottom of the second. One out, two balls, one strike. Johnny Cueto was shaky for the Reds and about to unravel in front of a mob of yinzers serenading him with a drawn-out call of his name. An inning after he'd let the Pirates open the scoring on a Marlon Byrd homer to left. Cueto paced around the rubber, dropped the ball as the crowd chanted, picked it back up and then left a belt-high fastball over the plate.

The roar when Russell Martin took Cueto way deep was the kind every fan should hear once in-person. Everyone in the park sensed it was gone off the bat, but the yells were tempered at first—these *were* the Pirates, and this was a big night and we *had* been burned enough times. When Ryan Ludwick ran out of space in left-center and the ball landed in a sea of black, *that's* when it became primal. That was the sound of the release when 39,000 people realize something is about to happen that hasn't happened in a long time. It was the sound of the longest streak of losing in major North American pro sports (*20 years*) becoming undone.

That night was a triumph. It was also the moment the Pirates stopped going up and started going down. Before the 2020 season, the Pirates cleaned house, finally getting rid of the last of the people who played meaningful roles in building them up to that night in 2013. In the last years of the last decade, the Pirates made a show of striving for mediocrity with a chance at lucking into something greater. But they didn't even make a cursory effort in perhaps the most variance-friendly season ever: a 60-game sprint before an expanded playoff.

The Pirates are the worst team in baseball entering 2021. They've been here before. This time, though, they've made sure their fanbase has no reason to believe in the rebuild to come.

The neat thing about being bad is that you are most likely on the way up; you're at least not on the way *down*. Being on the way up is exciting for a fan—albeit less so if you don't have a credible belief that you will then *stay* up.

The Pirates stayed up for a spell after 2013, the year the Cardinals beat them in five games in the Division Series. They were elite in both 2014 and 2015, when the misfortune of sharing a division with the Cardinals forced them into two more Wild Card Games. You know the story by now: they lost those games to peak Madison Bumgarner and peak Jake Arrieta. If they'd made another Wild Card Game, they probably would have faced a time-traveling Fernando Valenzuela. Sometimes things do not work out.

The Pirates had a young talent core after 2013. They stayed good the next two years despite not straying from newspaper magnate and team owner's Bob Nutting's established practice of avoiding aggressive major-league expenditures who would help the team stay relevant.

Nutting had authorized a few moves over the prior two years that qualified as lavish by the Pirates' standards: two years and $17 million for Martin, two years and $14 million for Franciso Liriano and picking up $13 million of the $31 million left on A.J. Burnett's Yankees deal. These commitments drew praise at the time, but more than that, they created more optimism than what would wind up being fulfilled.

The Pirates were a low-budget operation generations before Nutting's arrival. In 1950, Branch Rickey told Ralph Kiner he'd need to take a pay cut to stay with Pittsburgh, and when Kiner balked at the idea, Rickey told him, "We finished last with you. We can finish last without you." Then he traded him. Being cheap (or thrifty, depending on how you view labor-management dynamics) has long been a feature of the Pirates, and Nutting is only noteworthy because his net worth is measured in billions.

A loud camp of fans and local media couldn't stand Nutting's continual choice not to spend big, but some of us were okay with it—and even chastised *the non-believers* for not going along. After all, the Pirates could've spent $120 million on Matt Holliday in 2010 and been terrible anyway; better to conserve resources and get ready to spend to supplement a team that might be good once Nutting's underlings had built the farm system into something sustainable. Nutting and his team frequently alluded to a future in which the Pirates might invest more.

"A lot has been made of our payroll," then-GM Neal Huntington said that year, during a 105-loss campaign. "The easiest way to describe our payroll is that it's a result, not a goal—the result of trading players on the downside of their prime who were making a lot of money." Nutting, too, suggested the Pirates would pay up if the time were ever right: "Payroll is driven by the age and experience of those players. As those players mature, those dollars are going to need to mature with them. I think the payroll continues to be a distraction from the process of building the team."

It barely happened, outside of an eventual bargain extension for Andrew McCutchen and those big-for-the-Pirates value adds. The team went from 30th in Opening Day payroll in 2012 to 26th in 2013, then 28th in 2014, then 24th in

2015. They finished two games behind the Cardinals the latter two years and ran into pitching freight trains in the Wild Card Game both times. They jumped to 20th in 2016, but by that point they'd missed The Window, that period where low-spending teams have a chance to compete with their developed talent before it starts to cost a lot of money.

The realization the Pirates weren't going to supplement their elite teams of the early to mid-2010s with expensive outside acquisitions came gradually. It set in with each in a series of moves that could've made sense individually but added up to a clear betrayal of a fanbase that had been patient and expected some financial effort when the time was right. It was a slowly escalating deconstruction of a special team, with no serious effort at reinforcing it.

Ahead of 2016, they traded a productive second baseman (Neil Walker) for a bad starter (Jonathon Niese) because Walker was due to make at least $10 million in his last year arbitration. They saved less than $2 million to get 110 innings of sub-replacement-level mound work. Niese was supposed to help replace J.A. Happ, who'd provided a sub-2.00 ERA in 63 innings as a deadline pickup the year before, but he left for the Blue Jays when the Pirates wouldn't offer him more than two years. (Toronto offered three years and $36 million, which turned out to be a bargain). The Pirates' plan included spending $2 million on a 38-year-old Ryan Vogelsong, which went as you'd expect. They also made a poor attempt at Moneyballing by signing John Jaso (two years, $8 million) to play first base, a deal that returned less than one win in two seasons of regular starts. Jaso was, predictably, among the position's weakest hitters.

In 2017, cheapness blended with poor evaluation. The Pirates gave intermediate-sized deals to Francisco Cervelli, Iván Nova and David Freese, all contracts they'd later ship off. They also dumped the remainder of Liriano's contract on the Blue Jays, giving up two future major leaguers, Reese McGuire and Harold Ramirez, to do it. And as the season drew to a close, they let their second-best reliever, Juan Nicaso, go on an irrevocable waiver claim *to a division rival*, the Cardinals, without getting anything in return. At least it saved Nutting $600,000.

In 2018, with a surprisingly decent team, the Pirates made one of their versions of a "go for it" move—the kind of aggressive risk they liked to take to get a player who might be great and was on a good contract, so they wouldn't have to shell out for one in free agency. It wound up being one of the worst trades in recent baseball history: Chris Archer in, Tyler Glasnow and Austin Meadows (and more) out. You can't be stingy *and* bad at evaluating your own and others' talent.

Archer was supposed to replace Gerrit Cole, whom the Pirates misused and then traded with two years of club control remaining. Again, you can't be bad in too many ways all at once.

Ordinarily, there'd be room for some optimism now that Nutting has fired Huntington, the man chiefly responsible for all of those moves and non-moves. The Pirates were bad enough in 2020 to pick first in 2021's draft, in an era when it's not easy to botch the top pick as badly as, say, Dave Littlefield did when he took Bryan Bullington in 2002.

But every calamity Huntington inflicted on the Pirates was underpinned by Nutting's lack of interest in making the financial effort required to field a winner. And the Pirates replaced Huntington with Ben Cherington, as close to a Huntington clone as they could've found: in addition to nearly identical biographies that trace from New Hampshire upbringings to Amherst College to UMass to the Cleveland front office, Huntington helped Cherington get his start.

In swapping GMs, the Pirates have redecorated a shaky house without touching the foundation. Cherington may prove wiser than Huntington on his own terms—not trading Mitch Keller and Travis Swaggerty for a declining starter would be ideal—but he'll be constrained in similar ways. Even if he steers the ship wisely and gets the Pirates to contention by 2023, will he have any margin for error to keep them there beyond 2025? It's impossible to believe, and the slow bleed of the last great Pirates core has made it too painful to be worth investing hope.

Having a Scrooge of an owner is not unique. But Nutting exemplifies something unique about team-owner capitalism: the way it can take an opening and turn it into a peak. The way it can take a team on the rise, one a city falls deeply in love with, and then let it die on the vine. The way it can take the most joyful thing about sports, the journey, and make anyone on the ride live in constant fear of an elephant stepping out into the road.

The fun of the 2013-15 Pirates wasn't just that they'd been bad and were suddenly good. It was that they could *stay* good if the franchise thought it worthwhile. Sure, Bumgarner declares your pennant dreams dead on arrival one year. Sure, Arrieta does the same thing the next. There's no reason one of the best teams in baseball has to fall apart—unless the person signing the checks doesn't care to hold it together. It became exceedingly clear that Nutting did not care.

In this way, the Pirates' stinginess is a renewable poison. It has left a fanbase seething with anger over what could've been for those great McCutchen-era teams, of course, but it has also made it functionally impossible to believe in the long-range hopes of future good Pirates teams.

The Pirates also embark on this long rebuild with almost nothing of interest at the major-league level. The last Pirates team to be the worst in baseball was 2010's, but that team rolled out six starting position players who at least figured to have a chance of being significant players on their next contender. (It turns out three were, plus one starting pitcher.) The 2021 Pirates will start the year with *maybe* two or three useful pieces of the franchise's next good team on the roster, along with a number of veterans Cherington should've traded in his first months on the job. In addition to everything else, it isn't easy to watch these Pirates and feel inspiration.

The last time the team was this bad, years of mismanagement and not spending big had the bizarre effect of making the Pirates even more fun when the good times finally rolled. Part of it was the newness: the first time experiencing a packed ballpark on the shore of the Allegheny River every night, the first time seeing a whole caravan of Pirates in the All-Star Game, the first time seeing McCutchen on the cover of *Sports Illustrated*, the first time *Sunday Night Baseball* establishes a regular presence at your team's stadium. That feeling can never be felt again.

But part of the joy was the belief that success didn't have to be fleeting, because once a team builds something worth maintaining, maybe the guy in charge will do the work to sustain it. That feeling can also never be felt again. Nutting has lost any credibility that he will hold up his end of the bargain he made with Pirates fans who didn't quit long before that night in 2013, when Cueto dropped the ball. The owner has spent the rest of the decade dropping it himself.

—Alex Kirshner's work has appeared at The Ringer, Slate, SB Nation, and elsewhere.

Part 2: Player Analysis

PLAYER COMMENTS WITH GRAPHS

Phillip Evans 3B

Born: 09/10/92   Age: 28   Bats: R   Throws: R
Height: 5'10"   Weight: 215   Origin: Round 15, 2011 Draft (#462 overall)

YEAR	TEAM	LVL	AGE	PA	R	2B	3B	HR	RBI	BB	K	SB	CS	AVG/OBP/SLG
2018	LV	AAA	25	245	34	8	1	14	39	21	42	4	3	.256/.327/.493
2018	NYM	MLB	25	23	1	0	0	0	1	2	8	1	0	.143/.217/.143
2019	IOW	AAA	26	539	79	30	3	17	61	57	74	1	4	.283/.371/.470
2020	PIT	MLB	27	45	6	2	0	1	9	5	7	0	1	.359/.444/.487
2021 FS	PIT	MLB	28	600	66	27	2	17	70	47	131	0	1	.247/.315/.402
2021 DC	PIT	MLB	28	423	47	19	1	12	49	33	92	0	0	.247/.315/.402

Comparables: Brian Barden, Cristhian Adames, Matt Duffy

It took six long years for Evans to climb up the ladder of the Mets' minor league system before he met hitting coach Kevin Long, who helped him unlock his bat. That burgeoning power, combined with the same solid plate discipline he's shown throughout the minors, caught Pittsburgh's eye. The fact that the team was shy on utility players also helped, and he made the club out of spring training 2.0. Evans was off to his best start ever as a pro when he collided with outfielder Gregory Polanco while chasing a foul ball, breaking his jaw and ending his season. It's a shame, because Evans is the kind of feel-good success story Pirates fans could have used last year, but the next chapter will have to wait until this spring. (Un)luckily for Pirates fans, they'll probably still need to feel good then, too.

YEAR	TEAM	LVL	AGE	PA	DRC+	BABIP	BRR	FRAA	WARP
2018	LV	AAA	25	245	85	.255	-1.0	3B(22): -0.6, SS(19): -1.0, 2B(18): -3.4	-0.3
2018	NYM	MLB	25	23	73	.231	0.1	3B(3): -0.1, 2B(2): -0.0, 1B(1): 0.0	0.0
2019	IOW	AAA	26	539	110	.303	0.9	3B(95): -4.2, 1B(15): -0.2, 2B(15): 1.7	2.2
2020	PIT	MLB	27	45	104	.419	-0.1	3B(8): -0.8, 1B(1): -0.0, LF(1): -0.0	0.0
2021 FS	PIT	MLB	28	600	95	.295	-0.8	SS -1, 2B -1	0.6
2021 DC	PIT	MLB	28	423	95	.295	-0.6	SS -1, 2B -1	0.4

Phillip Evans, continued

Batted Ball Distribution

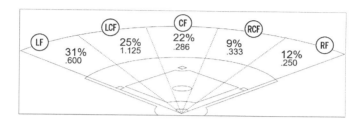

Strike Zone vs LHP   ## Strike Zone vs RHP

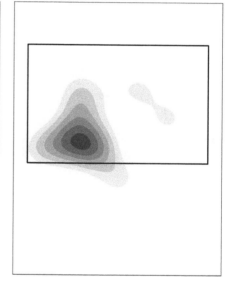

Adam Frazier   2B

Born: 12/14/91   Age: 29   Bats: L   Throws: R
Height: 5'10"   Weight: 180   Origin: Round 6, 2013 Draft (#179 overall)

YEAR	TEAM	LVL	AGE	PA	R	2B	3B	HR	RBI	BB	K	SB	CS	AVG/OBP/SLG
2018	IND	AAA	26	137	10	5	2	0	18	11	20	1	3	.223/.289/.298
2018	PIT	MLB	26	352	52	23	2	10	35	29	53	1	3	.277/.342/.456
2019	PIT	MLB	27	608	80	33	7	10	50	40	75	5	5	.278/.336/.417
2020	PIT	MLB	28	230	22	7	0	7	23	17	35	1	3	.230/.297/.364
2021 FS	PIT	MLB	29	600	74	31	5	13	57	47	97	8	6	.265/.336/.416
2021 DC	PIT	MLB	29	583	72	30	5	12	55	46	94	7	6	.265/.336/.416

Comparables: Ray Durham, Mark Ellis, D'Angelo Jimenez

Lefties who elevate do well at PNC Park with the short porch and Clemente Wall, and Frazier has parlayed that into 10-home run seasons over each of the past two years to go along with elite defense at second. The Pirates even gave him some outfield reps to gussy him up as a superutility for the trade deadline, but apparently the market was cold, likely due to him hitting the ball this season with all the impact of a Sternly Worded Email. With two more years of team control, he's one of Pittsburgh's better off-season trade chips, but his defensive chops could also help out a young pitching staff that's slightly above league average in groundball rate.

YEAR	TEAM	LVL	AGE	PA	DRC+	BABIP	BRR	FRAA	WARP
2018	IND	AAA	26	137	72	.262	-0.9	2B(17): 0.0, RF(7): -0.6, LF(5): 0.4	-0.4
2018	PIT	MLB	26	352	103	.305	1.7	2B(55): 2.5, LF(14): 0.7, RF(13): -0.6	1.6
2019	PIT	MLB	27	608	94	.306	1.0	2B(142): -6.4	1.1
2020	PIT	MLB	28	230	96	.246	0.9	2B(41): 0.5, LF(14): 1.9	1.0
2021 FS	PIT	MLB	29	600	102	.307	0.6	2B 0, LF 1	2.1
2021 DC	PIT	MLB	29	583	102	.307	0.6	2B 0, LF 1	2.0

Adam Frazier, continued

Batted Ball Distribution

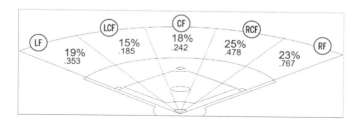

Strike Zone vs LHP

Strike Zone vs RHP

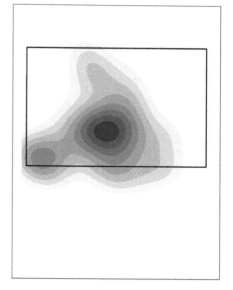

Erik González SS

Born: 08/31/91   Age: 29   Bats: R   Throws: R
Height: 6'3"   Weight: 205   Origin: International Free Agent, 2008

YEAR	TEAM	LVL	AGE	PA	R	2B	3B	HR	RBI	BB	K	SB	CS	AVG/OBP/SLG
2018	CLE	MLB	26	143	17	10	1	1	16	5	34	3	0	.265/.301/.375
2019	IND	AAA	27	81	6	3	1	1	10	3	29	1	1	.192/.222/.295
2019	PIT	MLB	27	156	15	4	1	1	6	9	37	4	1	.254/.301/.317
2020	PIT	MLB	28	193	14	13	1	3	20	8	51	2	3	.227/.255/.359
2021 FS	PIT	MLB	29	600	58	24	3	13	55	27	168	6	4	.222/.263/.350
2021 DC	PIT	MLB	29	419	40	17	2	9	39	19	117	4	3	.222/.263/.350

Comparables: Alex Gonzalez, Orlando Miller, Benji Gil

A hot start from the beginning of the season until mid-August plus solid defense at a premium position put some spice on his name at the trade deadline. But apparently the market was lukewarm, and rightfully so, as his performance over the remainder of the season proved. Defensive flexibility + speed + not a black hole at the plate = not a terrible utility-player profile. But given Pittsburgh's healthy supply of infielders and low relative demand for expertise, the 30-year-old González seems ticketed to be here for a moderately-okay time, not a long time.

YEAR	TEAM	LVL	AGE	PA	DRC+	BABIP	BRR	FRAA	WARP
2018	CLE	MLB	26	143	73	.347	1.9	2B(30): 2.0, 3B(20): 0.9, SS(16): 0.2	0.5
2019	IND	AAA	27	81	33	.292	-2.0	SS(9): -0.7, 2B(8): 0.8	-0.5
2019	PIT	MLB	27	156	65	.333	-0.1	SS(26): 1.4, 3B(16): 0.5, LF(4): -0.5	0.1
2020	PIT	MLB	28	193	74	.292	-1.0	SS(38): -2.2, 3B(13): 1.6	-0.2
2021 FS	PIT	MLB	29	600	64	.292	0.3	SS 0, 3B 1	-1.0
2021 DC	PIT	MLB	29	419	64	.292	0.2	SS 0, 3B 1	-0.6

Erik González, continued

Batted Ball Distribution

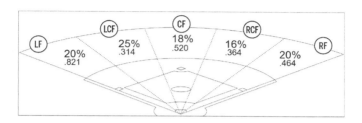

Strike Zone vs LHP   ## Strike Zone vs RHP

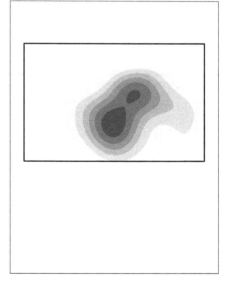

Brian Goodwin   LF

Born: 11/02/90   Age: 30   Bats: L   Throws: R
Height: 6'0"   Weight: 200   Origin: Round 1, 2011 Draft (#34 overall)

YEAR	TEAM	LVL	AGE	PA	R	2B	3B	HR	RBI	BB	K	SB	CS	AVG/OBP/SLG
2018	OMA	AAA	27	44	6	4	0	2	9	4	11	0	0	.225/.295/.475
2018	WAS	MLB	27	79	9	1	0	3	12	10	26	3	1	.200/.321/.354
2018	KC	MLB	27	101	11	5	0	3	13	6	31	1	1	.266/.317/.415
2019	LAA	MLB	28	458	65	29	3	17	47	38	129	7	3	.262/.326/.470
2020	CIN	MLB	29	55	5	2	0	2	5	5	19	4	0	.163/.236/.327
2020	LAA	MLB	29	109	12	7	1	4	17	12	35	1	0	.242/.330/.463
2021 FS	PIT	MLB	30	600	65	27	1	22	73	53	190	6	3	.223/.300/.402

Comparables: Pete Incaviglia, Geoff Jenkins, Marcus Thames

In the baseball equivalent the "it's not you, it's me" break-up, the Angels rewarded Goodwin's season-and-a-half of good work in their employ by shipping him off to Cincinnati at the deadline last summer for pitcher/Biggles character Packy Naughton in order to make more room for high-ceiling prospects Jo Adell and, eventually, Brandon Marsh. Predictably, Goodwin fell apart, scuffling along at the sub-replacement rate that has defined most of his career. A former Nats first rounder, Goodwin has a little power, a little speed, a little patience and a lot of track record painting him as a fourth outfielder with a poor hit tool who can't quite cover center field.

YEAR	TEAM	LVL	AGE	PA	DRC+	BABIP	BRR	FRAA	WARP
2018	OMA	AAA	27	44	88	.259	0.1	CF(3): -0.5, LF(2): 0.9, RF(2): -0.4	0.0
2018	WAS	MLB	27	79	80	.270	-1.8	LF(11): -0.2, RF(10): -0.7, CF(7): 0.1	-0.2
2018	KC	MLB	27	101	83	.367	0.2	CF(25): -0.7, LF(1): -0.1	0.1
2019	LAA	MLB	28	458	99	.337	-1.3	LF(68): -4.0, CF(39): -3.7, RF(17): 4.1	0.9
2020	CIN	MLB	29	55	86	.207	0.5	CF(16): -2.4, LF(2): -0.0, RF(1): -0.0	-0.1
2020	LAA	MLB	29	109	92	.333	0.6	LF(14): -1.2, RF(11): 2.3, CF(4): 0.1	0.2
2021 FS	PIT	MLB	30	600	86	.303	-0.2	CF -1, LF 0	0.6

Brian Goodwin, continued

Batted Ball Distribution

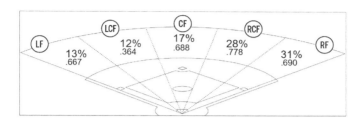

Strike Zone vs LHP   ## Strike Zone vs RHP

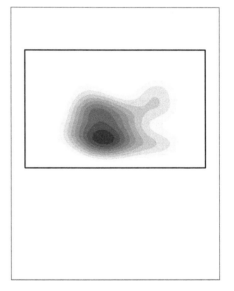

Ke'Bryan Hayes   3B

Born: 01/28/97   Age: 24   Bats: R   Throws: R
Height: 5'10"   Weight: 205   Origin: Round 1, 2015 Draft (#32 overall)

YEAR	TEAM	LVL	AGE	PA	R	2B	3B	HR	RBI	BB	K	SB	CS	AVG/OBP/SLG
2018	ALT	AA	21	508	64	31	7	7	47	57	84	12	5	.293/.375/.444
2019	IND	AAA	22	480	64	30	2	10	53	43	90	12	1	.265/.336/.415
2020	PIT	MLB	23	95	17	7	2	5	11	9	20	1	0	.376/.442/.682
2021 FS	PIT	MLB	24	600	72	30	5	14	65	52	139	7	2	.254/.327/.414
2021 DC	PIT	MLB	24	570	68	29	5	14	62	49	132	6	2	.254/.327/.414

Comparables: Andy Marte, Ian Stewart, Willy Aybar

"You are always new," wrote poet John Keats to Fanny Brawne in 1820, and 200 years later, the sentiment is echoed among Pirates fans marveling over their exciting young rookie. A positive COVID-19 test kept him from making his debut until September, but the son of former Pirate Charlie Hayes was electric, unveiling a new aspect to his game each night: dazzling snags at third; a mature approach in the box, especially with two strikes; smart and speedy baserunning; an ability to hit to all fields; and tantalizing flashes of power in the bat. With a tooled-up skillset and a billboard-ready smile, Hayes the Younger is the kind of player long-suffering Pirates fans can dream on, and deserve to love as a "joy forever."

YEAR	TEAM	LVL	AGE	PA	DRC+	BABIP	BRR	FRAA	WARP
2018	ALT	AA	21	508	128	.344	-0.8	3B(116): 9.0	3.5
2019	IND	AAA	22	480	96	.311	2.3	3B(104): 8.2	2.3
2020	PIT	MLB	23	95	115	.450	0.6	3B(24): 3.0	0.7
2021 FS	PIT	MLB	24	600	102	.317	0.3	3B 4	1.7
2021 DC	PIT	MLB	24	570	102	.317	0.3	3B 4	1.6

Ke'Bryan Hayes, continued

Batted Ball Distribution

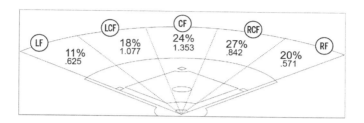

Strike Zone vs LHP   **Strike Zone vs RHP**

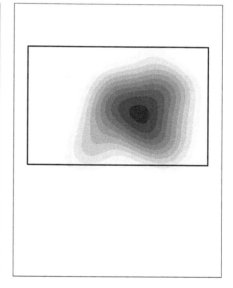

Colin Moran   3B

Born: 10/01/92   Age: 28   Bats: L   Throws: R
Height: 6'4"   Weight: 220   Origin: Round 1, 2013 Draft (#6 overall)

YEAR	TEAM	LVL	AGE	PA	R	2B	3B	HR	RBI	BB	K	SB	CS	AVG/OBP/SLG
2018	PIT	MLB	25	465	49	19	1	11	58	39	82	0	2	.277/.340/.407
2019	PIT	MLB	26	503	46	30	1	13	80	30	117	0	1	.277/.322/.429
2020	PIT	MLB	27	200	28	10	0	10	23	19	52	0	0	.247/.325/.472
2021 FS	PIT	MLB	28	600	70	28	2	20	74	52	153	0	1	.245/.320/.418
2021 DC	PIT	MLB	28	493	57	23	1	16	61	43	125	0	1	.245/.320/.418

Comparables: David Freese, Kevin Kouzmanoff, Eric Munson

Like a frozen french bread pizza heated up by the drunkest person at the party, he was hot at the ends and ice-cold in the middle of the truncated season. Moran walks up to "Start Me Up," by the Stones, an appropriate throwback for a player who looks like he belongs on a three-color baseball card. And perhaps that fueled his hot start, as he was the first player to five homers, reaching that mark on the first of August. He'd then wait another two weeks before hitting another, and only tally four more over the remainder of the season, two in the last four games. To be fair, those weeks were marked with many stops and starts for the Pirates due to the pandemic, making it hard for Moran to hit his stride. He'd end the season strong, with the kind of Three-True-Outcomes line that makes his full-time move to first a palatable one, value-wise.

YEAR	TEAM	LVL	AGE	PA	DRC+	BABIP	BRR	FRAA	WARP
2018	PIT	MLB	25	465	99	.316	-1.5	3B(116): -2.7	1.2
2019	PIT	MLB	26	503	84	.341	-0.7	3B(121): -18.7, 2B(11): 0.1, 1B(8): -0.4	-1.1
2020	PIT	MLB	27	200	103	.291	-0.6	1B(22): 0.7, 3B(4): -0.3	0.3
2021 FS	PIT	MLB	28	600	97	.308	-0.8	1B 1, 2B 0	1.0
2021 DC	PIT	MLB	28	493	97	.308	-0.6	1B 1	0.6

Colin Moran, continued

Batted Ball Distribution

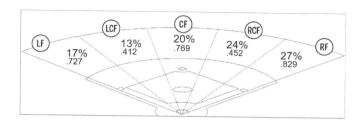

Strike Zone vs LHP

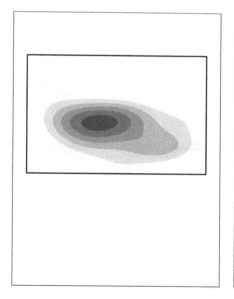

Strike Zone vs RHP

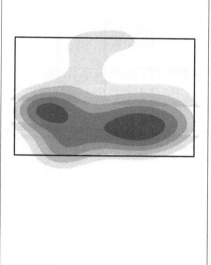

Kevin Newman   SS

Born: 08/04/93   Age: 27   Bats: R   Throws: R
Height: 6'0"   Weight: 185   Origin: Round 1, 2015 Draft (#19 overall)

YEAR	TEAM	LVL	AGE	PA	R	2B	3B	HR	RBI	BB	K	SB	CS	AVG/OBP/SLG
2018	IND	AAA	24	477	74	30	2	4	35	31	50	28	11	.302/.350/.407
2018	PIT	MLB	24	97	7	2	0	0	6	4	23	0	1	.209/.247/.231
2019	IND	AAA	25	35	5	2	0	0	1	5	7	0	1	.233/.343/.300
2019	PIT	MLB	25	531	61	20	6	12	64	28	62	16	8	.308/.353/.446
2020	PIT	MLB	26	172	12	5	0	1	10	12	21	0	1	.224/.281/.276
2021 FS	PIT	MLB	27	600	68	29	3	11	57	38	90	8	4	.268/.322/.393
2021 DC	PIT	MLB	27	203	23	10	1	3	19	13	30	2	2	.268/.322/.393

Comparables: Jimmy Rollins, Angel Berroa, Zoilo Versalles

The good: Newman once again proved allergic to striking out, carrying that part of his 2019 breakthrough forward. The bad: literally everything else, as the regression monster came to collect on an inflated slash line belied by weak batted-ball data. The ugly: continued defensive struggles up the middle, and a pre-pitch routine slightly less rhythmic than the dinner party scene in *Beetlejuice*. Newman claims an abdominal injury suffered in late August didn't affect his play, but he lost over a hundred points on his slash line across the board after being lifted from the game with discomfort. He wasn't hitting the ball hard before, but after, he might as well have been swinging a soggy Pixy Stix at the plate. That's bad news for a player whose value is tied to his bat, so hopefully the injury was actually the culprit, and Newman can take the off-season to heal, sort out his twitchy pre-pitch routine, and live to fight another Day-O.

YEAR	TEAM	LVL	AGE	PA	DRC+	BABIP	BRR	FRAA	WARP
2018	IND	AAA	24	477	122	.333	3.2	SS(83): 2.9, 2B(21): -0.6	3.0
2018	PIT	MLB	24	97	61	.275	-0.6	SS(24): -1.4, 2B(8): -0.7	-0.3
2019	IND	AAA	25	35	84	.304	0.7	SS(4): -0.4, LF(2): -0.3, CF(2): 0.0	0.1
2019	PIT	MLB	25	531	106	.333	0.9	SS(104): -1.3, 2B(23): -0.0, 3B(6): 0.5	2.8
2020	PIT	MLB	26	172	86	.250	-0.5	SS(23): -0.9, 2B(20): 0.5	0.1
2021 FS	PIT	MLB	27	600	97	.303	0.3	SS 0, 2B 0	1.6
2021 DC	PIT	MLB	27	203	97	.303	0.1	SS 0, 2B 0	0.5

Kevin Newman, continued

Batted Ball Distribution

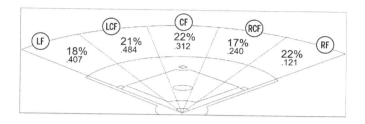

Strike Zone vs LHP   Strike Zone vs RHP

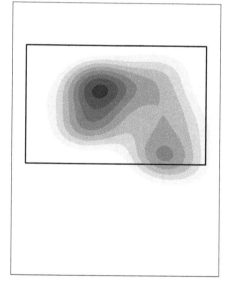

José Osuna   3B

Born: 12/12/92   Age: 28   Bats: R   Throws: R
Height: 6'2"   Weight: 235   Origin: International Free Agent, 2009

YEAR	TEAM	LVL	AGE	PA	R	2B	3B	HR	RBI	BB	K	SB	CS	AVG/OBP/SLG
2018	IND	AAA	25	342	45	26	0	9	59	31	51	5	3	.321/.378/.497
2018	PIT	MLB	25	111	14	9	0	3	11	3	22	0	0	.226/.252/.396
2019	IND	AAA	26	83	13	7	1	2	13	9	22	2	0	.268/.361/.479
2019	PIT	MLB	26	285	41	20	0	10	36	18	48	0	0	.264/.310/.456
2020	PIT	MLB	27	82	6	3	0	4	11	4	16	0	1	.205/.244/.397
2021 FS	PIT	MLB	28	600	65	32	2	22	75	38	126	0	1	.247/.301/.434

Comparables: Lance Niekro, Ken Harvey, Brian R. Hunter

Osuna is your friend who shows up to the barbecue with two bags of ice right when you've run out; he's good in a pinch. He's also your friend who is only good in a pinch—you didn't assign them more than two bags of ice for a reason, and the party would go on without him. Osuna can't tolerate more exposure to quality pitching without his flaws in the field and at the plate becoming readily apparent. He's a reliable guy, but not one you want to rely on too much, unless your team, like his new one, makes its home in Tokyo.

YEAR	TEAM	LVL	AGE	PA	DRC+	BABIP	BRR	FRAA	WARP
2018	IND	AAA	25	342	156	.353	1.4	3B(47): 4.6, 1B(24): -0.7, RF(9): 2.7	3.4
2018	PIT	MLB	25	111	79	.256	0.8	1B(12): 1.9, 3B(7): -0.2, RF(7): 0.1	0.3
2019	IND	AAA	26	83	113	.354	0.2	RF(12): -2.6, LF(3): -0.2, 1B(1): -0.0	0.1
2019	PIT	MLB	26	285	93	.285	-1.1	1B(31): 1.2, RF(23): -0.5, 3B(19): 1.0	0.6
2020	PIT	MLB	27	82	93	.207	-0.7	1B(9): -0.3, RF(7): 0.4, 3B(5): 0.3	0.1
2021 FS	PIT	MLB	28	600	96	.284	-0.8	3B 1, 1B 0	0.8

José Osuna, continued

Batted Ball Distribution

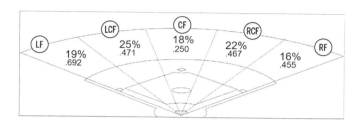

Strike Zone vs LHP

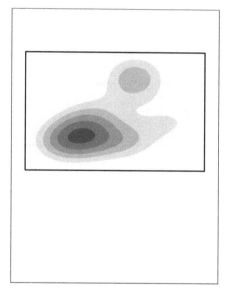

Strike Zone vs RHP

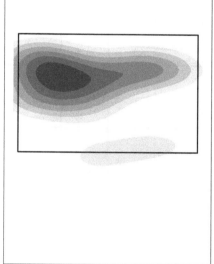

Michael Perez   C

Born: 08/07/92   Age: 28   Bats: L   Throws: R
Height: 5'10"   Weight: 195   Origin: Round 5, 2011 Draft (#154 overall)

YEAR	TEAM	LVL	AGE	PA	R	2B	3B	HR	RBI	BB	K	SB	CS	AVG/OBP/SLG
2018	RNO	AAA	25	240	30	9	1	6	29	20	40	0	1	.284/.342/.417
2018	TB	MLB	25	80	9	5	0	1	11	3	19	0	0	.284/.304/.392
2019	DUR	AAA	26	216	23	7	0	13	42	28	51	0	2	.245/.338/.495
2019	TB	MLB	26	55	6	5	0	0	2	8	19	0	0	.217/.345/.326
2020	TB	MLB	27	93	7	3	0	1	13	7	27	0	0	.167/.237/.238
2021 FS	PIT	MLB	28	600	65	27	2	18	63	50	174	0	1	.220/.292/.378
2021 DC	PIT	MLB	28	262	28	11	1	8	27	22	76	0	0	.220/.292/.378

Comparables: Tim Laudner, Ron Karkovice, Ben Davis

The Pirates claimed Perez off waivers from the Rays shortly after the World Series. He's just a backup catcher, albeit one freshly christened with Postseason Success.

YEAR	TEAM	P. COUNT	FRM RUNS	BLK RUNS	THRW RUNS	TOT RUNS
2018	TB	3023	-3.5	0.5	0.0	-2.9
2019	TB	2100	0.1	0.9	-0.2	0.7
2020	TB	3701	-1.3	-0.2	-0.1	-1.6
2021	PIT	10822	-5.8	1.1	0.4	-4.3
2021	PIT	10822	-5.8	-0.7	0.4	-6.1

YEAR	TEAM	LVL	AGE	PA	DRC+	BABIP	BRR	FRAA	WARP
2018	RNO	AAA	25	240	97	.322	-1.3	C(57): 8.7	1.6
2018	TB	MLB	25	80	87	.357	-1.8	C(24): -3.6	-0.3
2019	DUR	AAA	26	216	116	.258	0.9	C(44): 1.2	1.5
2019	TB	MLB	26	55	73	.370	-1.2	C(20): 0.9, 1B(2): 0.0	0.1
2020	TB	MLB	27	93	76	.228	-0.8	C(38): 0.8, 1B(1): 0.1	0.0
2021 FS	PIT	MLB	28	600	79	.291	-0.8	C -6, 1B 0	0.1
2021 DC	PIT	MLB	28	262	79	.291	-0.3	C -4	-0.1

Michael Perez, continued

Batted Ball Distribution

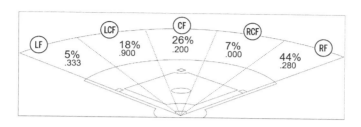

Strike Zone vs LHP   Strike Zone vs RHP

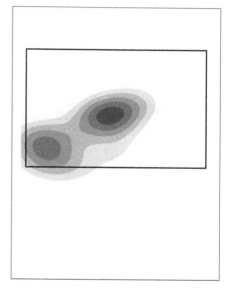

Gregory Polanco RF

Born: 09/14/91   Age: 29   Bats: L   Throws: L
Height: 6'5"   Weight: 235   Origin: International Free Agent, 2009

YEAR	TEAM	LVL	AGE	PA	R	2B	3B	HR	RBI	BB	K	SB	CS	AVG/OBP/SLG
2018	PIT	MLB	26	535	75	32	6	23	81	61	117	12	2	.254/.340/.499
2019	IND	AAA	27	54	5	4	0	1	11	9	16	2	0	.267/.389/.422
2019	PIT	MLB	27	167	23	8	1	6	17	12	49	3	1	.242/.301/.425
2020	PIT	MLB	28	174	12	6	0	7	22	13	65	3	1	.153/.214/.325
2021 FS	PIT	MLB	29	600	68	29	3	22	72	56	176	12	4	.223/.302/.416
2021 DC	PIT	MLB	29	487	55	24	2	18	59	45	143	9	4	.223/.302/.416

Comparables: Brennan Boesch, Derek Bell, Dave Clark

He's always late on fastballs, but his penitence is real He can't make solid contact, you can't count on him to steal We hate to have to say it, but we very firmly feel Polanco's not an asset to the Pirates

(We'd like to say a word on his behalf: You can't blame him ... for the pitching staff)

How do you solve a problem like Polanco Eleven million owed, to be quite blunt How do you solve a problem like Polanco? A swing change? A PED? More bunts?

Oh, how do you trade a player like Polanco? [MUSIC SWELLS] Pray the Yankees fall back in the hunt

YEAR	TEAM	LVL	AGE	PA	DRC+	BABIP	BRR	FRAA	WARP
2018	PIT	MLB	26	535	106	.287	0.7	RF(124): 1.3	1.8
2019	IND	AAA	27	54	111	.393	1.0	RF(8): -1.1	0.2
2019	PIT	MLB	27	167	79	.316	0.5	RF(36): 0.4	0.0
2020	PIT	MLB	28	174	73	.193	-0.8	RF(39): 2.0	-0.1
2021 FS	PIT	MLB	29	600	89	.291	0.8	RF 2	0.7
2021 DC	PIT	MLB	29	487	89	.291	0.6	RF 1	0.5

Gregory Polanco, continued

Batted Ball Distribution

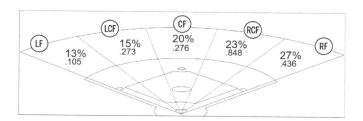

Strike Zone vs LHP

Strike Zone vs RHP

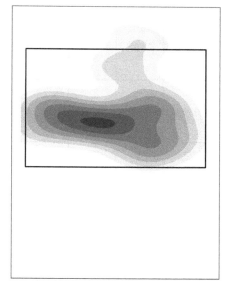

Bryan Reynolds   LF

Born: 01/27/95   Age: 26   Bats: S   Throws: R
Height: 6'3"   Weight: 205   Origin: Round 2, 2016 Draft (#59 overall)

YEAR	TEAM	LVL	AGE	PA	R	2B	3B	HR	RBI	BB	K	SB	CS	AVG/OBP/SLG
2018	ALT	AA	23	383	56	18	3	7	46	43	73	4	4	.302/.381/.438
2019	IND	AAA	24	57	10	1	1	5	11	7	11	3	2	.367/.446/.735
2019	PIT	MLB	24	546	83	37	4	16	68	46	121	3	2	.314/.377/.503
2020	PIT	MLB	25	208	24	6	2	7	19	21	57	1	1	.189/.275/.357
2021 FS	PIT	MLB	26	600	75	26	5	20	71	54	164	1	1	.251/.326/.430
2021 DC	PIT	MLB	26	568	71	24	4	19	67	51	155	1	1	.251/.326/.430

Comparables: Justin Upton, Marty Cordova, Chris Heisey

"Sophomore slump" doesn't begin to cover the tumble Reynolds' bat took between his standout rookie year and 2020, but there are still things to like in this profile. He's still barreling up the ball and hitting line drives to all fields, even if he's not hitting it quite as hard as last season; his low BABIP suggests a certain amount of bad luck, given the exit velo and line drive rate; and he's shown himself to be a solid defender in center. Not a burner on the bases, Reynolds is nonetheless a smart runner who can take the extra base and does all the little things well. The profile has all the sex appeal of a sloth in a Speedo, but it's a perfectly serviceable one. It'll likely look even better next season, once his strikeout percentage settles back down to career levels after a feverish spike caused by an acute case of Trying To Do Too Much for the offensively punchless Pirates.

YEAR	TEAM	LVL	AGE	PA	DRC+	BABIP	BRR	FRAA	WARP
2018	ALT	AA	23	383	133	.362	-0.2	CF(43): -3.2, LF(42): -3.6, RF(3): 1.3	1.3
2019	IND	AAA	24	57	178	.394	-0.7	CF(13): -1.3	0.5
2019	PIT	MLB	24	546	110	.387	1.5	LF(79): -0.4, RF(31): 0.1, CF(25): -1.9	2.2
2020	PIT	MLB	25	208	86	.231	-2.2	LF(37): 1.2, CF(17): 0.9	0.5
2021 FS	PIT	MLB	26	600	105	.326	-0.2	LF 1, CF 0	2.2
2021 DC	PIT	MLB	26	568	105	.326	-0.2	LF 1, CF 0	2.1

Bryan Reynolds, continued

Batted Ball Distribution

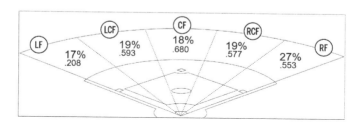

Strike Zone vs LHP

Strike Zone vs RHP

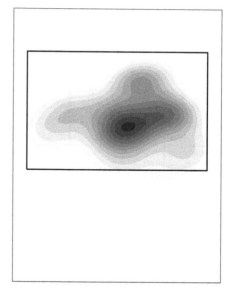

Jacob Stallings   C

Born: 12/22/89   Age: 31   Bats: R   Throws: R
Height: 6'5"   Weight: 215   Origin: Round 7, 2012 Draft (#226 overall)

YEAR	TEAM	LVL	AGE	PA	R	2B	3B	HR	RBI	BB	K	SB	CS	AVG/OBP/SLG
2018	IND	AAA	28	278	37	22	1	3	40	15	51	1	2	.285/.335/.414
2018	PIT	MLB	28	41	2	0	0	0	5	3	9	0	0	.216/.268/.216
2019	IND	AAA	29	61	11	9	0	2	7	4	9	0	0	.275/.361/.569
2019	PIT	MLB	29	210	26	5	0	6	13	16	40	0	0	.262/.325/.382
2020	PIT	MLB	30	143	13	7	0	3	18	15	40	0	0	.248/.326/.376
2021 FS	PIT	MLB	31	600	60	23	1	16	62	39	161	1	1	.217/.279/.351
2021 DC	PIT	MLB	31	270	27	10	0	7	27	17	72	0	0	.217/.279/.351

Comparables: Dave Duncan, Ramon Castro, Cal Neeman

Behold the field in which the Pirates grow their catchers, and see that it is barren. A career backup who was a senior sign in 2012, Stallings ascended to the starting job after free agent signee Luke Maile went down with a broken finger during summer camp. Proving that 6'4" is not too tall for a catcher, he was again one of the best

YEAR	TEAM	P. COUNT	FRM RUNS	BLK RUNS	THRW RUNS	TOT RUNS
2018	PIT	1479	-0.7	0.5	0.0	-0.2
2018	IND	8836	-6.1	0.3	-0.1	-6.0
2019	PIT	7741	8.7	3.6	0.3	12.6
2019	IND	2150	0.9	0.0	0.1	1.0
2020	PIT	6186	2.7	1.1	-0.1	3.7
2021	PIT	10822	1.0	1.7	0.3	3.0
2021	PIT	10822	1.0	3.4	0.3	4.7

behind the dish this season, tying for the lead in the NL in runners caught stealing along with exceptional framing abilities and softer hands than a Victorian debutante. He wasn't a black hole at the plate, either, and would have led the Pirates in WARP if not for the emergence of Ke'Bryan Hayes. By the end of the season he was the team's Roberto Clemente Award nominee and a Gold Glove candidate, which is quite the glow-up for a player twice waived and cleared. He works well with this developing pitching staff and will likely continue to do so until the Pirates invest in a legitimate starting catching option, either in the draft or free agency or by propping a lululemon bag with a string tied to it over a Chipotle burrito.

YEAR	TEAM	LVL	AGE	PA	DRC+	BABIP	BRR	FRAA	WARP
2018	IND	AAA	28	278	116	.343	-1.4	C(63): -4.7	0.8
2018	PIT	MLB	28	41	74	.276	0.5	C(13): 0.1	0.1
2019	IND	AAA	29	61	115	.286	-3.2	C(15): 0.6	0.2
2019	PIT	MLB	29	210	95	.303	0.6	C(61): 13.6, P(1): -0.0	2.3
2020	PIT	MLB	30	143	96	.337	-1.0	C(42): 1.3	0.8
2021 FS	PIT	MLB	31	600	71	.277	-0.8	C 9, 1B 0	1.0
2021 DC	PIT	MLB	31	270	71	.277	-0.3	C 5	0.6

Jacob Stallings, continued

Batted Ball Distribution

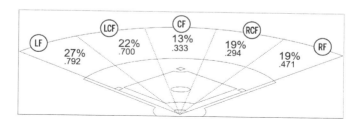

Strike Zone vs LHP

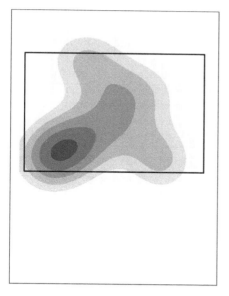

Strike Zone vs RHP

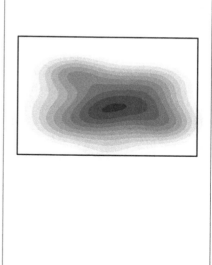

Cole Tucker SS

Born: 07/03/96   Age: 25   Bats: S   Throws: R
Height: 6'3"   Weight: 205   Origin: Round 1, 2014 Draft (#24 overall)

YEAR	TEAM	LVL	AGE	PA	R	2B	3B	HR	RBI	BB	K	SB	CS	AVG/OBP/SLG
2018	ALT	AA	21	589	77	21	7	5	44	55	104	35	12	.259/.333/.356
2019	IND	AAA	22	353	51	15	4	8	28	38	73	11	3	.261/.346/.413
2019	PIT	MLB	22	159	16	10	3	2	13	10	40	0	0	.211/.266/.361
2020	PIT	MLB	23	116	17	3	0	1	8	5	31	1	0	.220/.252/.275
2021 FS	PIT	MLB	24	600	63	26	6	11	56	45	157	12	6	.229/.293/.363
2021 DC	PIT	MLB	24	348	36	15	3	6	32	26	91	7	3	.229/.293/.363

Comparables: Alex Gonzalez, Felipe Lopez, Darrel Chaney

If one were to pen a cliché pop-country song about Tucker, it'd probably mention something about "long legs and bad decisions." On the surface, these both seem undeniable: the teeny-tiny walk rate compared to the much larger strikeout rate, and the fact that whoever designed his lower half had a heavy hand on the knee-to-hip ratio dial, or just had extra left over after making Nick Madrigal. But Tucker's swing decisions are mostly average to good. The problem is he struggles to make contact, and when he does, the quality of that contact has been poor. It's too early to worry about a player with fewer than 400 career PAs, especially since the Pirates tossed him into the outfield, where he fared well in both right and center despite being a dirt-dweller his whole career. Long legs are cliché for a reason: they get things done, but we'd like to see those legs used better in Tucker's top-heavy swing. Tucker did spend the 2020 off-season working on creating more loft in his swing path and moving his hands to keep his bat on plane in the zone longer, but those adjustments hadn't yet shown up at the plate before his season ended prematurely due to concussion.

YEAR	TEAM	LVL	AGE	PA	DRC+	BABIP	BRR	FRAA	WARP
2018	ALT	AA	21	589	90	.310	3.4	SS(131): -0.6	1.3
2019	IND	AAA	22	353	102	.319	1.2	SS(70): -4.7, 2B(6): 0.8	1.3
2019	PIT	MLB	22	159	62	.276	1.3	SS(45): -1.1	0.0
2020	PIT	MLB	23	116	60	.295	0.1	CF(20): -1.5, RF(16): -0.9, 2B(1): -0.0	-0.6
2021 FS	PIT	MLB	24	600	78	.302	1.4	CF -7, RF -3	-0.8
2021 DC	PIT	MLB	24	348	78	.302	0.8	CF -4, RF -2	-0.5

Cole Tucker, continued

Batted Ball Distribution

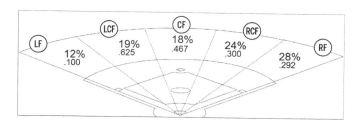

Strike Zone vs LHP   ## *Strike Zone vs RHP*

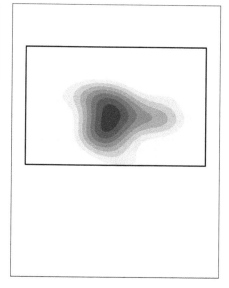

Steven Brault   LHP

Born: 04/29/92   Age: 29   Bats: L   Throws: L
Height: 6'0"   Weight: 195   Origin: Round 11, 2013 Draft (#339 overall)

YEAR	TEAM	LVL	AGE	W	L	SV	G	GS	IP	H	HR	BB/9	K/9	K	GB%	BABIP
2018	IND	AAA	26	0	1	0	5	0	5^1	6	0	6.8	11.8	7	40.0%	.400
2018	PIT	MLB	26	6	3	0	45	5	91^2	84	10	5.6	8.1	82	47.0%	.292
2019	PIT	MLB	27	4	6	0	25	19	113^1	117	15	4.2	7.9	100	42.7%	.313
2020	PIT	MLB	28	1	3	0	11	10	42^2	29	2	4.6	8.0	38	49.6%	.243
2021 FS	PIT	MLB	29	9	9	0	26	26	150	147	21	4.7	8.5	141	46.4%	.299
2021 DC	PIT	MLB	29	7	8	0	24	25	119	116	17	4.7	8.5	112	46.4%	.299

Comparables: Chris Stratton, Alec Mills, Adam Plutko

The Final Boss of the Pirates' Pitchers With Personality rotation, the heavily-tattooed Brault is not content to show off by himself, but likes to get his teammates in on the act. He hosts a podcast with Trevor Williams, and Josh Bell appears on the album of Broadway covers he released last spring. However, the results on the mound have been middling until recently, when new pitching coach Oscar Marin adjusted Brault's pitch mix to feature less of his toothsome four-seamer, which he used to throw about half the time, and instead lean more heavily on his secondaries, especially a grounder-inducing changeup. But the biggest change Marin made was encouraging Brault to stop poring over scouting reports and instead trust his catcher to call the game while he focused solely on executing pitches. It may be antithetical to an actor, but giving focus away seems to have worked for Brault, whose last two starts of the season were the best of his Pirates career. As with everything else in 2020, it's small sample size theater, but then again, the the-ah-tre is where Brault is the most comfortable.

YEAR	TEAM	LVL	AGE	WHIP	ERA	DRA-	WARP	MPH	FB%	WHF	CSP
2018	IND	AAA	26	1.88	3.38	79	0.1				
2018	PIT	MLB	26	1.54	4.61	126	-0.7	94.7	65.0%	24.5%	
2019	PIT	MLB	27	1.50	5.16	90	1.6	93.8	64.3%	23.3%	
2020	PIT	MLB	28	1.20	3.38	109	0.2	94.2	50.7%	23.9%	
2021 FS	PIT	MLB	29	1.50	5.08	109	0.6	94.1	60.6%	23.7%	46.1%
2021 DC	PIT	MLB	29	1.50	5.08	109	0.4	94.1	60.6%	23.7%	46.1%

Steven Brault, continued

Pitch Shape vs LHH

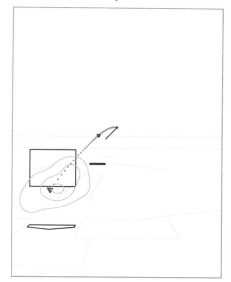

Pitch Shape vs RHH

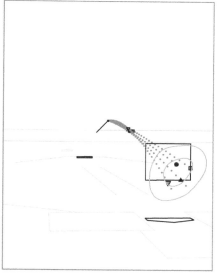

Type		Frequency	Velocity	H Movement	V Movement
●	Fastball	39.0%	92.5 [100]	7.5 [96]	-15.1 [100]
□	Sinker	11.7%	91.5 [95]	12.4 [105]	-21.8 [96]
▲	Changeup	24.3%	85.2 [100]	11.1 [103]	-30.6 [92]
▽	Slider	22.5%	83.2 [97]	-5.6 [101]	-36.9 [91]

JT Brubaker   RHP

Born: 11/17/93   Age: 27   Bats: R   Throws: R
Height: 6'3"   Weight: 185   Origin: Round 6, 2015 Draft (#187 overall)

YEAR	TEAM	LVL	AGE	W	L	SV	G	GS	IP	H	HR	BB/9	K/9	K	GB%	BABIP
2018	ALT	AA	24	2	2	0	6	6	35	29	1	2.1	9.0	35	61.2%	.289
2018	IND	AAA	24	8	4	0	22	22	119	121	7	2.7	7.3	96	49.0%	.323
2019	WV	SS	25	0	0	0	2	2	6^2	5	0	5.4	5.4	4	42.1%	.263
2019	IND	AAA	25	2	1	0	4	4	21	19	2	1.7	8.6	20	52.5%	.298
2020	PIT	MLB	26	1	3	0	11	9	47^1	48	6	3.2	9.1	48	47.4%	.321
2021 FS	PIT	MLB	27	9	8	0	26	26	150	143	20	3.3	8.4	139	48.4%	.295
2021 DC	PIT	MLB	27	5	5	0	11	19	85.3	81	11	3.3	8.4	79	48.4%	.295

Comparables: Keury Mella, Chris Stratton, Walker Lockett

The 26-year-old rookie Brubaker has a rainforest-lush beard and deeply haunted eyes, eyes that have Seen Things, those Things apparently being the David Lynch joint known as the 2020 Pirates. Between a lack of prospect pedigree and missing most of 2019 with a forearm strain, he's about as under-the-radar as it gets, but there's late-inning potential here as a reliever who can touch 98 paired with a hard slider-cutter hybrid. As a starter, the fastball velocity drops slightly, but only into the 94-95 range, with above-average spin dotted at the top and bottom of the zone with late movement; alongside the scythe-like slider he adds a high-spin curveball that's been graded as average-plus but attracted significant whiffs in a limited MLB sample size. On the mound he comes right at hitters, working at a pace that suggests the game interrupted him mid-Netflix binge. Fantasy players should snatch him up on the cheap; the Eyes are not what they seem.

YEAR	TEAM	LVL	AGE	WHIP	ERA	DRA-	WARP	MPH	FB%	WHF	CSP
2018	ALT	AA	24	1.06	1.80	60	1.0				
2018	IND	AAA	24	1.32	3.10	89	1.5				
2019	WV	SS	25	1.35	1.35	112	0.0				
2019	IND	AAA	25	1.10	2.57	58	0.8				
2020	PIT	MLB	26	1.37	4.94	85	0.8	95.7	49.8%	27.6%	
2021 FS	PIT	MLB	27	1.32	4.28	96	1.8	95.7	49.8%	27.6%	45.2%
2021 DC	PIT	MLB	27	1.32	4.28	96	1.0	95.7	49.8%	27.6%	45.2%

JT Brubaker, continued

Pitch Shape vs LHH

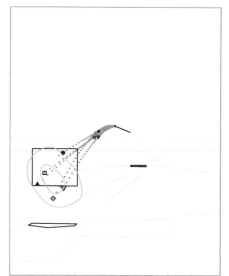

Pitch Shape vs RHH

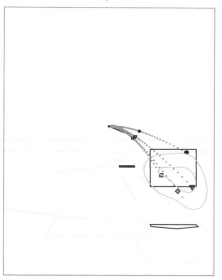

Type		Frequency	Velocity	H Movement	V Movement
●	Fastball	14.3%	93.6 [103]	-7 [98]	-15 [100]
□	Sinker	35.4%	94 [108]	-14.1 [92]	-19.2 [104]
▲	Changeup	4.0%	88 [111]	-12.1 [98]	-25.3 [106]
▽	Slider	32.5%	87.7 [117]	1.4 [85]	-29.3 [113]
◇	Curveball	13.7%	80.8 [108]	7.3 [99]	-44.4 [109]

Carson Fulmer RHP

Born: 12/13/93   Age: 27   Bats: R   Throws: R
Height: 6'0"   Weight: 215   Origin: Round 1, 2015 Draft (#8 overall)

YEAR	TEAM	LVL	AGE	W	L	SV	G	GS	IP	H	HR	BB/9	K/9	K	GB%	BABIP
2018	CHA	AAA	24	5	6	0	25	9	67²	70	10	5.5	8.2	62	38.5%	.321
2018	CHW	MLB	24	2	4	0	9	8	32¹	37	8	6.7	8.1	29	33.0%	.299
2019	CHA	AAA	25	1	2	1	24	0	34	31	2	5.6	13.5	51	32.5%	.372
2019	CHW	MLB	25	1	2	0	20	2	27¹	26	5	6.6	8.2	25	45.9%	.263
2020	PIT	MLB	26	0	0	0	10	0	10¹	8	1	4.4	9.6	11	53.6%	.259
2021 FS	PIT	MLB	27	2	3	0	57	0	50	45	8	5.5	9.5	52	40.3%	.287
2021 DC	PIT	MLB	27	1	1	0	31	0	54.3	49	8	5.5	9.5	57	40.3%	.287

Comparables: Chase De Jong, Lucas Sims, Robert Stephenson

After thunking around the waiver wire like a plinko chip, Fulmer landed in Pittsburgh for a second time, which is good, as it has potential to benefit both sides. As a high-profile former top draft pick widely considered a bust, molding Fulmer into an effective major-league reliever would be a feather in the cap of the Pirates' new analytics-friendly regime and a sign that the don't-call-it-a-rebuild might plod along at a slightly less ponderous pace. For Fulmer, the literal poster child for why excessive head whack is considered undesirable in pitching prospects, he gets not only a fresh start, but also a Dorothy-in-Oz experience of what experiences are available outside the world of black-and-white.

YEAR	TEAM	LVL	AGE	WHIP	ERA	DRA-	WARP	MPH	FB%	WHF	CSP
2018	CHA	AAA	24	1.64	5.32	150	-1.5				
2018	CHW	MLB	24	1.89	8.07	180	-1.0	94.4	55.3%	18.3%	
2019	CHA	AAA	25	1.53	4.76	70	0.9				
2019	CHW	MLB	25	1.68	6.26	135	-0.4	95.3	43.9%	24.3%	
2020	PIT	MLB	26	1.26	4.35	73	0.2	93.7	54.3%	32.5%	
2021 FS	PIT	MLB	27	1.51	5.09	108	0.0	94.7	49.6%	24.6%	44.7%
2021 DC	PIT	MLB	27	1.51	5.09	108	0.1	94.7	49.6%	24.6%	44.7%

Carson Fulmer, continued

Pitch Shape vs LHH

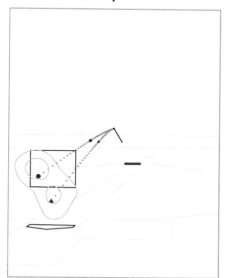

Pitch Shape vs RHH

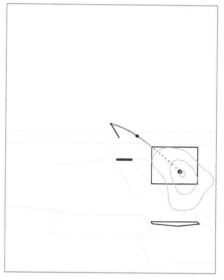

Type	Frequency	Velocity	H Movement	V Movement
● Fastball	54.3%	92.5 [100]	-7.1 [98]	-15 [101]
+ Cutter	11.7%	86.3 [87]	4.8 [119]	-30.8 [74]
▲ Changeup	22.9%	86.1 [104]	-12.1 [98]	-30.6 [91]
◇ Curveball	11.2%	81.5 [111]	5.1 [90]	-42.7 [113]

Geoff Hartlieb   RHP

Born: 12/09/93   Age: 27   Bats: R   Throws: R
Height: 6'5"   Weight: 240   Origin: Round 29, 2016 Draft (#885 overall)

YEAR	TEAM	LVL	AGE	W	L	SV	G	GS	IP	H	HR	BB/9	K/9	K	GB%	BABIP
2018	ALT	AA	24	8	2	10	47	0	58¹	56	3	3.7	8.6	56	61.7%	.325
2019	IND	AAA	25	4	1	3	26	0	39²	31	0	3.4	11.3	50	63.3%	.316
2019	PIT	MLB	25	0	1	0	29	0	35	52	8	4.6	9.8	38	45.2%	.415
2020	PIT	MLB	26	1	0	0	21	0	22¹	16	1	7.7	7.7	19	60.0%	.254
2021 FS	PIT	MLB	27	2	2	0	57	0	50	46	5	5.0	9.1	50	54.0%	.302
2021 DC	PIT	MLB	27	2	2	0	44	0	54.3	50	6	5.0	9.1	54	54.0%	.302

Comparables: John Curtiss, Phil Maton, Yacksel Ríos

Born with an extra bone in his foot, Hartlieb spent his first year in the bigs pitching in constant pain. He had offsesason surgery prior to 2020 to address it, but then had to readjust his mechanics accordingly. Hartlieb's Instagram bio describes him as a "seasonal employee of the Pittsburgh Pirates," but the Pirates seem poised to count on him full-time next year.

YEAR	TEAM	LVL	AGE	WHIP	ERA	DRA-	WARP	MPH	FB%	WHF	CSP
2018	ALT	AA	24	1.37	3.24	78	0.8				
2019	IND	AAA	25	1.16	2.50	53	1.4				
2019	PIT	MLB	25	2.00	9.00	104	0.1	98.1	70.4%	23.3%	
2020	PIT	MLB	26	1.57	3.63	98	0.2	95.9	53.5%	24.9%	
2021 FS	PIT	MLB	27	1.48	4.62	100	0.2	97.0	62.3%	24.1%	47.5%
2021 DC	PIT	MLB	27	1.48	4.62	100	0.3	97.0	62.3%	24.1%	47.5%

Geoff Hartlieb, continued

Pitch Shape vs LHH

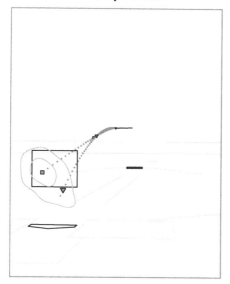

Pitch Shape vs RHH

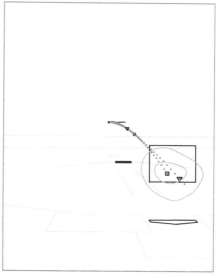

Type	Frequency	Velocity	H Movement	V Movement
□ Sinker	53.5%	93.8 [107]	-13.9 [94]	-22.2 [94]
▽ Slider	45.5%	82.9 [95]	10.6 [120]	-37.8 [88]

Derek Holland LHP

Born: 10/09/86   Age: 34   Bats: S   Throws: L
Height: 6'2"   Weight: 213   Origin: Round 25, 2006 Draft (#748 overall)

YEAR	TEAM	LVL	AGE	W	L	SV	G	GS	IP	H	HR	BB/9	K/9	K	GB%	BABIP
2018	SF	MLB	31	7	9	0	36	30	171¹	154	19	3.5	8.9	169	39.6%	.294
2019	SF	MLB	32	2	4	0	31	7	68²	68	17	4.6	9.3	71	41.4%	.291
2019	CHC	MLB	32	0	1	0	20	1	15²	14	3	5.7	6.3	11	36.2%	.256
2020	PIT	MLB	33	1	3	0	12	5	40²	42	12	3.3	10.0	45	37.1%	.288
2021 FS	*PIT*	*MLB*	*34*	*2*	*3*	*0*	*57*	*0*	*50*	*48*	*8*	*3.5*	*8.6*	*47*	*39.5%*	*.290*
2021 DC	*PIT*	*MLB*	*34*	*3*	*3*	*0*	*68*	*0*	*59*	*57*	*9*	*3.5*	*8.6*	*56*	*39.5%*	*.290*

Comparables: Iván Nova, Homer Bailey, Matt Shoemaker

Wanting to improve on a lousy 2019, when he lost control of his slider and had to rely heavily on his sinker, Holland did all the right things. He hooked up with old friend pitching coach Oscar Marin, whom he knew from the Rangers organization, signed a minor-league deal with the Pirates, showed up to camp and assumed the role of Veteran Leader. Marin, well-versed in the art of retreads from two years as the Mariners' MiLB pitching coordinator in 2017-18, had Holland increase his changeup usage, pairing it with an uptick in throwing his four-seamer at the top of the zone as well as at the bottom, and added some more horizontal movement to his 12-6 slider. It didn't work, thanks partly to an outrageously high HR/FB%, which will happen when you throw a bunch of mediocre four-seamers up in the zone. Still, you have to admire the 33-year-old for trying, as well as for being the first active MLB player ejected from the stands during his team's game. Suck it, Strasburg.

YEAR	TEAM	LVL	AGE	WHIP	ERA	DRA-	WARP	MPH	FB%	WHF	CSP
2018	SF	MLB	31	1.29	3.57	84	2.9	93.3	56.9%	24.0%	
2019	SF	MLB	32	1.50	5.90	143	-1.1	94.5	60.9%	27.5%	
2019	CHC	MLB	32	1.53	6.89	48	0.5	95.3	67.4%	22.5%	
2020	PIT	MLB	33	1.40	6.86	147	-0.7	93.8	46.7%	26.5%	
2021 FS	*PIT*	*MLB*	*34*	*1.37*	*4.58*	*107*	*0.1*	*94.0*	*56.1%*	*25.7%*	*48.1%*
2021 DC	*PIT*	*MLB*	*34*	*1.37*	*4.58*	*107*	*0.2*	*94.0*	*56.1%*	*25.7%*	*48.1%*

Derek Holland, continued

Pitch Shape vs LHH

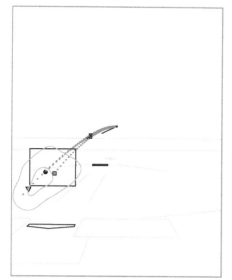

Pitch Shape vs RHH

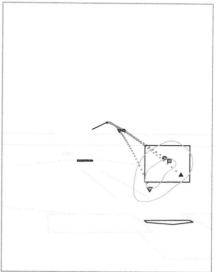

Type		Frequency	Velocity	H Movement	V Movement
●	Fastball	17.5%	92.5 [100]	12.7 [71]	-15.4 [99]
□	Sinker	29.2%	92.6 [101]	14.5 [90]	-17.5 [110]
▲	Changeup	15.9%	84.5 [98]	10.8 [105]	-20.8 [118]
▽	Slider	36.6%	81 [87]	-0.4 [82]	-35.5 [95]

Sam Howard LHP

Born: 03/05/93   Age: 28   Bats: R   Throws: L
Height: 6'4"   Weight: 190   Origin: Round 3, 2014 Draft (#82 overall)

YEAR	TEAM	LVL	AGE	W	L	SV	G	GS	IP	H	HR	BB/9	K/9	K	GB%	BABIP
2018	ABQ	AAA	25	3	8	0	21	21	96	106	13	3.2	7.5	80	36.7%	.332
2018	COL	MLB	25	0	0	0	4	0	4	5	0	6.8	2.2	1	53.3%	.333
2019	ABQ	AAA	26	4	1	1	42	0	50²	50	5	4.1	11.0	62	44.2%	.363
2019	COL	MLB	26	2	0	0	20	0	19	21	5	4.7	10.9	23	38.2%	.333
2020	PIT	MLB	27	2	3	0	22	0	21	17	4	3.9	11.6	27	29.4%	.277
2021 FS	*PIT*	*MLB*	*28*	*2*	*2*	*0*	*57*	*0*	*50*	*44*	*7*	*3.6*	*9.7*	*53*	*37.5%*	*.290*
2021 DC	*PIT*	*MLB*	*28*	*2*	*2*	*0*	*44*	*0*	*54.3*	*48*	*8*	*3.6*	*9.7*	*58*	*37.5%*	*.290*

Comparables: Steven Brault, Erick Fedde, Cody Reed

Howard is a long-limbed crossfire lefty with a fastball-slider combo who pitches like an atomic-age starburst clock that wished to be a real baseball player, but got monkey-pawed into the 2020 Pirates bullpen instead. That still might be preferable to pitching in Colorado, which is where the Pirates claimed him from, and his numbers did trend in a moderately more positive direction in Pittsburgh, netting a few more whiffs overall. What's most interesting about Howard isn't him as a player but as a bellwether of the current player development in Pittsburgh, indicating the Pirates are able to pick up waiver wire dross and magic it up into gold, or at least in this case, polished brass.

YEAR	TEAM	LVL	AGE	WHIP	ERA	DRA-	WARP	MPH	FB%	WHF	CSP
2018	ABQ	AAA	25	1.46	5.06	104	0.7				
2018	COL	MLB	25	2.00	2.25	189	-0.2	92.3	48.8%	17.0%	
2019	ABQ	AAA	26	1.44	3.91	61	1.6				
2019	COL	MLB	26	1.63	6.63	80	0.3	94.2	44.1%	32.8%	
2020	PIT	MLB	27	1.24	3.86	105	0.1	93.6	37.4%	35.8%	
2021 FS	*PIT*	*MLB*	*28*	*1.30*	*4.14*	*93*	*0.4*	*93.8*	*40.6%*	*33.8%*	*40.6%*
2021 DC	*PIT*	*MLB*	*28*	*1.30*	*4.14*	*93*	*0.5*	*93.8*	*40.6%*	*33.8%*	*40.6%*

Sam Howard, continued

Pitch Shape vs LHH

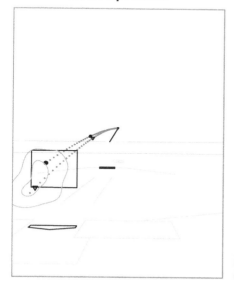

Pitch Shape vs RHH

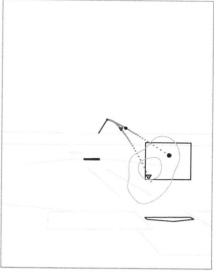

Type	Frequency	Velocity	H Movement	V Movement
● Fastball	37.4%	92.3 [99]	8.6 [91]	-12.8 [107]
▽ Slider	62.3%	84.8 [104]	-1.8 [87]	-28.9 [114]

Mitch Keller   RHP

Born: 04/04/96   Age: 25   Bats: R   Throws: R
Height: 6'2"   Weight: 210   Origin: Round 2, 2014 Draft (#64 overall)

YEAR	TEAM	LVL	AGE	W	L	SV	G	GS	IP	H	HR	BB/9	K/9	K	GB%	BABIP
2018	ALT	AA	22	9	2	0	14	14	86	64	7	3.3	8.0	76	53.8%	.252
2018	IND	AAA	22	3	2	0	10	10	52^1	59	3	3.8	9.8	57	32.7%	.368
2019	IND	AAA	23	7	5	0	19	19	103^2	94	9	3.0	10.7	123	43.2%	.331
2019	PIT	MLB	23	1	5	0	11	11	48	72	6	3.0	12.2	65	39.3%	.478
2020	PIT	MLB	24	1	1	0	5	5	21^2	9	4	7.5	6.6	16	42.3%	.104
2021 FS	PIT	MLB	25	9	8	0	26	26	150	140	21	4.2	8.9	149	42.2%	.295
2021 DC	PIT	MLB	25	8	8	0	24	25	129.3	121	18	4.2	8.9	128	42.2%	.295

Comparables: Jake Faria, Zac Gallen, Griffin Canning

IL stints were up across MLB in 2020, but the luckless Pirates seemed to fall out of the Injury Tree and hit all the branches on the way down. The worst sting for future-focused Pirates fans was the loss of their top pitching prospect to an oblique injury after just two starts. For Keller, he lost precious development time as he continued to adjust to the more-discerning eyes of MLB batters. After his fastball got hit around in his debut year, Keller worked more on spinning it up in the zone in 2020, but more often than not wound up sailing lower-velocity fastballs up towards the cardboard cutout fans. It also affected his best secondary in his 12-6 curve, which lost a good deal of its plus drop and wasn't as effective a weapon. Keller looked much better in his return from the IL, with his fastball zooming up to 96-98, but consistency will be required for him to earn the money and fame accorded a frontline starter. Avoiding injuries and global pandemics is a good place to start.

YEAR	TEAM	LVL	AGE	WHIP	ERA	DRA-	WARP	MPH	FB%	WHF	CSP
2018	ALT	AA	22	1.12	2.72	80	1.6				
2018	IND	AAA	22	1.55	4.82	81	0.9				
2019	IND	AAA	23	1.24	3.56	69	3.3				
2019	PIT	MLB	23	1.83	7.12	85	0.8	97.3	59.5%	26.6%	
2020	PIT	MLB	24	1.25	2.91	135	-0.2	96.6	55.9%	21.2%	
2021 FS	PIT	MLB	25	1.41	4.58	100	1.5	97.0	57.9%	24.2%	45.6%
2021 DC	PIT	MLB	25	1.41	4.58	100	1.3	97.0	57.9%	24.2%	45.6%

Mitch Keller, continued

Pitch Shape vs LHH

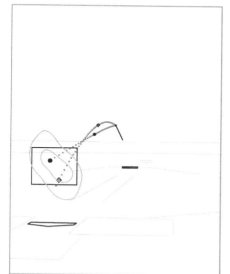

Pitch Shape vs RHH

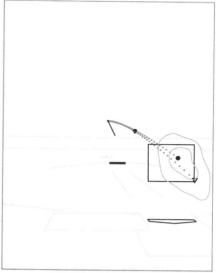

Type	Frequency	Velocity	H Movement	V Movement
● Fastball	55.9%	94.2 [105]	-6.3 [102]	-12.8 [107]
▲ Changeup	3.1%	89.1 [115]	-11.8 [99]	-23.6 [111]
▽ Slider	21.7%	87.2 [114]	3.7 [94]	-28.1 [116]
◇ Curveball	19.3%	78.4 [99]	7 [98]	-52.8 [90]

Chad Kuhl   RHP

Born: 09/10/92   Age: 28   Bats: R   Throws: R
Height: 6'3"   Weight: 210   Origin: Round 9, 2013 Draft (#269 overall)

YEAR	TEAM	LVL	AGE	W	L	SV	G	GS	IP	H	HR	BB/9	K/9	K	GB%	BABIP
2018	PIT	MLB	25	5	5	0	16	16	85	89	14	3.5	8.6	81	36.5%	.319
2020	PIT	MLB	27	2	3	0	11	9	46¹	35	8	5.4	8.5	44	41.8%	.239
2021 FS	PIT	MLB	28	9	9	0	26	26	150	142	24	4.1	8.8	146	42.6%	.290
2021 DC	PIT	MLB	28	7	7	0	25	22	113.3	107	18	4.1	8.8	110	42.6%	.290

Comparables: Taijuan Walker, Michael Fulmer, Zach Davies

In his much-anticipated return from TJ surgery, Kuhl displayed the consistency of an oatmeal sandwich for much of the season. The challenge of returning from a major injury and the attendant downtick in stuff as he built innings, combined with a shortened, start-and-stop season and a nagging torn fingernail on his pitching hand, added up to a performance that can be wiped away in favor of a fresh start in '21. New pitching coach Oscar Marin has shown he's not afraid to toy with pitchers' arsenals, but that hasn't yet borne out in Kuhl's offerings. He's still throwing his sinking fastball 42 percent of the time, and it got hit hard (6 HR, .667 SLG), though he was much improved after a midseason IL stint. Kuhl Hand believers will note his best start of the year was his last one, when he blanked the Cubs over seven innings.

YEAR	TEAM	LVL	AGE	WHIP	ERA	DRA-	WARP	MPH	FB%	WHF	CSP
2018	PIT	MLB	25	1.44	4.55	94	1.0	97.2	59.0%	23.6%	
2020	PIT	MLB	27	1.36	4.27	115	0.0	95.9	43.9%	27.0%	
2021 FS	PIT	MLB	28	1.41	4.73	104	1.1	96.4	49.6%	25.7%	46.2%
2021 DC	PIT	MLB	28	1.41	4.73	104	0.8	96.4	49.6%	25.7%	46.2%

Chad Kuhl, continued

Pitch Shape vs LHH

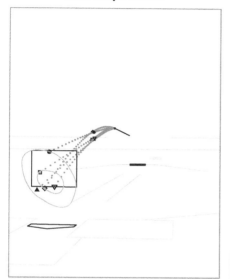

Pitch Shape vs RHH

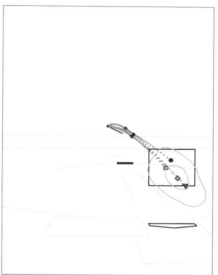

Type		Frequency	Velocity	H Movement	V Movement
●	Fastball	8.4%	93.9 [104]	-8.9 [89]	-14.6 [102]
□	Sinker	35.5%	94.2 [109]	-11.9 [109]	-17 [111]
▲	Changeup	4.1%	88.4 [113]	-12.3 [97]	-27.2 [101]
▽	Slider	35.4%	87.9 [118]	3.5 [94]	-29.6 [112]
◇	Curveball	16.7%	81.4 [111]	8.6 [104]	-44.5 [109]

Dovydas Neverauskas RHP

Born: 01/14/93   Age: 28   Bats: R   Throws: R
Height: 6'3"   Weight: 225   Origin:

YEAR	TEAM	LVL	AGE	W	L	SV	G	GS	IP	H	HR	BB/9	K/9	K	GB%	BABIP
2018	IND	AAA	25	2	3	4	34	0	46¹	31	2	5.8	11.3	58	48.5%	.290
2018	PIT	MLB	25	0	0	0	25	0	27	30	9	3.3	9.0	27	37.0%	.292
2019	IND	AAA	26	3	4	9	36	0	52	51	8	3.8	12.6	73	37.2%	.358
2019	PIT	MLB	26	0	0	0	10	0	9¹	15	2	6.8	9.6	10	35.3%	.406
2020	PIT	MLB	27	0	3	0	17	0	19	24	5	4.7	10.9	23	46.4%	.373
2021 FS	PIT	MLB	28	2	2	0	57	0	50	44	7	4.5	10.1	55	41.3%	.294

Comparables: Jake Barrett, Yacksel Ríos, J.B. Wendelken

Fans of the global game of baseball have a soft spot for Neverauskas as the first Lithuanian-born MLB player, but a second straight year of underachieving numbers had even the most loyal yinzers rumbling. The Pirates, always happy to listen to their fanbase (when it involves cutting payroll), designated Nerverauskas this November. He soon found a home with NPB's Hiroshima Toyo Carp. His struggles are perplexing because the stuff looks fine on paper, a mid-90s fastball paired with a changing-speed cutter and a hard curve; however, batters have crushed said fastball, mostly thanks to his propensity to throw it right down the heart of the plate. To his credit, he did cut the usage of his four-seamer from 57 percent to 48, which in our opinion is still too high given that batters slugged 1.000 off of it, but hey, they never ask us.

YEAR	TEAM	LVL	AGE	WHIP	ERA	DRA-	WARP	MPH	FB%	WHF	CSP
2018	IND	AAA	25	1.32	2.53	69	0.9				
2018	PIT	MLB	25	1.48	8.00	107	0.0	98.6	48.1%	27.4%	
2019	IND	AAA	26	1.40	5.02	89	0.9				
2019	PIT	MLB	26	2.36	10.61	129	-0.1	97.6	57.1%	28.0%	
2020	PIT	MLB	27	1.79	7.11	94	0.2	96.3	46.4%	32.5%	
2021 FS	PIT	MLB	28	1.39	4.39	97	0.3	97.2	49.1%	30.2%	44.3%

Dovydas Neverauskas, continued

Pitch Shape vs LHH

Pitch Shape vs RHH

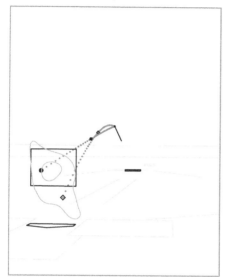
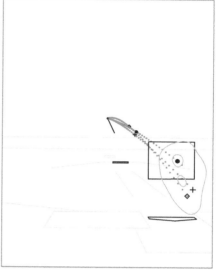

Type	Frequency	Velocity	H Movement	V Movement
● Fastball	46.4%	94.9 [107]	-6.8 [99]	-10.9 [112]
+ Cutter	19.6%	89.8 [109]	3.5 [110]	-23 [105]
◇ Curveball	33.8%	82.3 [114]	5.5 [91]	-47.4 [102]

Cody Ponce RHP

Born: 04/25/94   Age: 27   Bats: R   Throws: R
Height: 6'6"   Weight: 255   Origin: Round 2, 2015 Draft (#55 overall)

YEAR	TEAM	LVL	AGE	W	L	SV	G	GS	IP	H	HR	BB/9	K/9	K	GB%	BABIP
2018	BLX	AA	24	7	6	0	29	11	95	88	10	3.2	8.3	88	43.6%	.294
2019	ALT	AA	25	0	0	1	3	1	6	3	1	1.5	9.0	6	40.0%	.143
2019	BLX	AA	25	1	3	1	27	0	38^1	33	1	2.8	10.3	44	54.5%	.330
2019	IND	AAA	25	1	3	0	4	4	18^2	18	4	3.4	9.6	20	52.7%	.275
2020	PIT	MLB	26	1	1	0	5	3	17	12	5	3.2	6.4	12	35.4%	.163
2021 FS	PIT	MLB	27	2	2	0	57	0	50	46	8	3.3	8.0	44	42.8%	.279
2021 DC	PIT	MLB	27	4	3	0	22	8	52.7	49	8	3.3	8.0	47	42.8%	.279

Comparables: Asher Wojciechowski, Wes Parsons, Erick Fedde

If you're looking at your favorite team's rotation and wondering why they all boast the personality of a wafer cookie, it's because the Pirates are hogging all of the fun pitchers. Mustachioed, merry and a little mischievous, Ponce's persona is more colorful than his stuff, although some dream of moving "The Big Fella" to the 'pen where his fastball could play into the upper 90s paired with a hard, slider-ish cutter that wipes out lefties. But Ponce impressed in a rotation audition, showcasing an ability to spot both the fastball and the cutter all over the zone, along with an average curve that has swing-and-miss potential and a changeup he spent quarantine improving. He might have the prototypical wacky reliever sense of humor, but everything else about this profile feels back-end starter-like, at least until proven otherwise.

YEAR	TEAM	LVL	AGE	WHIP	ERA	DRA-	WARP	MPH	FB%	WHF	CSP
2018	BLX	AA	24	1.28	4.36	85	1.3				
2019	ALT	AA	25	0.67	6.00	63	0.1				
2019	BLX	AA	25	1.17	3.29	90	0.1				
2019	IND	AAA	25	1.34	5.30	81	0.5				
2020	PIT	MLB	26	1.06	3.18	144	-0.2	94.7	68.3%	19.1%	
2021 FS	PIT	MLB	27	1.30	4.35	98	0.3	94.7	68.3%	19.1%	48.8%
2021 DC	PIT	MLB	27	1.30	4.35	98	0.5	94.7	68.3%	19.1%	48.8%

Cody Ponce, continued

Pitch Shape vs LHH

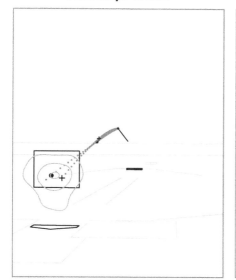

Pitch Shape vs RHH

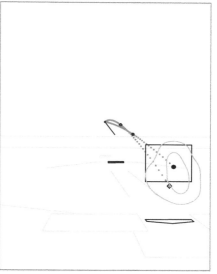

Type	Frequency	Velocity	H Movement	V Movement
● Fastball	42.6%	93.6 [103]	-9.1 [88]	-13.8 [104]
+ Cutter	24.5%	89.6 [108]	1.9 [100]	-21.7 [110]
▲ Changeup	7.9%	84.9 [99]	-12.8 [94]	-24.5 [108]
◇ Curveball	23.8%	78.6 [100]	7 [98]	-49.6 [97]

Richard Rodríguez RHP

Born: 03/04/90   Age: 31   Bats: R   Throws: R
Height: 6'4"   Weight: 220   Origin: International Free Agent, 2010

YEAR	TEAM	LVL	AGE	W	L	SV	G	GS	IP	H	HR	BB/9	K/9	K	GB%	BABIP
2018	IND	AAA	28	0	0	0	2	0	5	1	0	3.6	16.2	9	14.3%	.143
2018	PIT	MLB	28	4	3	0	63	0	69¹	55	5	2.5	11.4	88	35.9%	.311
2019	PIT	MLB	29	4	5	1	72	0	65¹	65	14	3.2	8.7	63	43.7%	.280
2020	PIT	MLB	30	3	2	4	24	0	23¹	15	3	1.9	13.1	34	38.5%	.250
2021 FS	PIT	MLB	31	2	2	14	57	0	50	41	7	2.6	10.4	57	38.9%	.282
2021 DC	PIT	MLB	31	2	2	14	57	0	61.3	50	8	2.6	10.4	71	38.9%	.282

Comparables: Paul Sewald, Andrew Kittredge, Jacob Barnes

Pittsburgh had two of the top 50 relievers in a year where bullpens were inventing new ways to shave years off fans' lives, so it's weird that both of them finished the year as Pirates, especially as both are 30-year-olds just now entering their first year of arbitration. Of the two, Rodríguez has more of the late-inning profile, with a high-spin fastball/slider combo. He doubled said slider usage in 2020 and saw an attendant rise in whiffs, ranking in the top five percent of all pitchers in strikeout percentage, but also dabbled dangerously with hard-hit balls when the breaking pitches didn't break. It's possible some poor outings right at the deadline colored league perception, or maybe Ben Cherington set the price too high, but dealing neither pitcher at the deadline feels like a missed opportunity both for the team and for fans around the league who white-knuckled their way through late innings in the playoffs.

YEAR	TEAM	LVL	AGE	WHIP	ERA	DRA-	WARP	MPH	FB%	WHF	CSP
2018	IND	AAA	28	0.60	0.00	16	0.2				
2018	PIT	MLB	28	1.07	2.47	63	1.7	94.5	75.1%	30.9%	
2019	PIT	MLB	29	1.35	3.72	96	0.5	94.8	85.2%	23.9%	
2020	PIT	MLB	30	0.86	2.70	76	0.5	94.5	72.4%	36.0%	
2021 FS	PIT	MLB	31	1.12	3.32	78	0.9	94.7	79.5%	28.7%	48.2%
2021 DC	PIT	MLB	31	1.12	3.32	78	1.1	94.7	79.5%	28.7%	48.2%

Richard Rodríguez, continued

Pitch Shape vs LHH

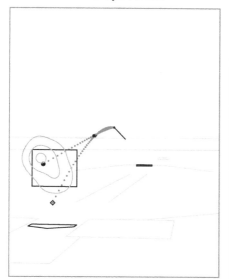

Pitch Shape vs RHH

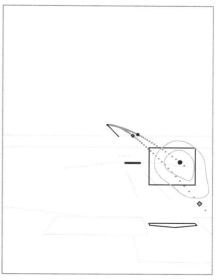

Type	Frequency	Velocity	H Movement	V Movement
● Fastball	72.2%	93.2 [102]	-11.8 [76]	-14.2 [103]
◇ Curveball	27.6%	81.5 [111]	6 [94]	-41.5 [115]

Chasen Shreve LHP

Born: 07/12/90   Age: 30   Bats: L   Throws: L
Height: 6'4"   Weight: 195   Origin: Round 11, 2010 Draft (#344 overall)

YEAR	TEAM	LVL	AGE	W	L	SV	G	GS	IP	H	HR	BB/9	K/9	K	GB%	BABIP
2018	NYY	MLB	27	2	2	1	40	0	38	39	8	4.3	10.9	46	48.6%	.320
2018	STL	MLB	27	1	2	0	20	0	14²	14	3	5.5	9.8	16	20.0%	.297
2019	MEM	AAA	28	2	2	3	51	0	60	45	6	3.9	10.1	67	29.7%	.273
2019	STL	MLB	28	1	0	0	3	0	2	2	0	4.5	9.0	2	0.0%	.333
2020	NYM	MLB	29	1	0	0	17	0	25	17	4	4.3	12.2	34	39.3%	.250
2021 FS	PIT	MLB	30	2	2	0	57	0	50	42	8	4.4	11.0	61	37.2%	.289

Comparables: Shawn Armstrong, Nick Wittgren, Tommy Kahnle

Shreve made the most of his NRI and nailed down the "second lefty" spot on the Mets' roster, which seems to be about right for someone with his profile. With him, there tends to be a little too much of everything: too many homers and walks for his team's liking, to go with plenty of strikeouts for the opposing hitters. Though his effectiveness waned in September, he was one of the Mets' most reliable relief arms during the short season. Despite more strikeouts than any reliever except Edwin Díaz and the third-most innings of anyone in the New York bullpen, the Mets non-tendered him in the offseason because of another too much: his price tag in arbitration.

YEAR	TEAM	LVL	AGE	WHIP	ERA	DRA-	WARP	MPH	FB%	WHF	CSP
2018	NYY	MLB	27	1.50	4.26	63	0.9	93.4	52.9%	33.1%	
2018	STL	MLB	27	1.57	3.07	120	-0.1	93.3	56.1%	31.0%	
2019	MEM	AAA	28	1.18	3.45	52	2.1				
2019	STL	MLB	28	1.50	9.00	121	0.0	91.3	66.7%	10.5%	
2020	NYM	MLB	29	1.16	3.96	81	0.5	92.9	51.2%	37.8%	
2021 FS	PIT	MLB	30	1.34	4.15	93	0.4	93.1	52.8%	34.6%	40.2%

Chasen Shreve, continued

Pitch Shape vs LHH

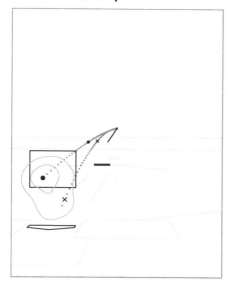

Pitch Shape vs RHH

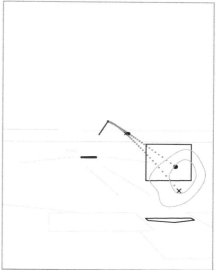

Type		Frequency	Velocity	H Movement	V Movement
●	Fastball	51.2%	91.9 [98]	9.3 [88]	-13.2 [106]
✕	Splitter	40.8%	83.5 [92]	11.8 [86]	-30.3 [97]
▽	Slider	8.1%	80 [82]	-5.3 [100]	-44.5 [69]

Chris Stratton   RHP

Born: 08/22/90   Age: 30   Bats: R   Throws: R
Height: 6'2"   Weight: 205   Origin: Round 1, 2012 Draft (#20 overall)

YEAR	TEAM	LVL	AGE	W	L	SV	G	GS	IP	H	HR	BB/9	K/9	K	GB%	BABIP
2018	SAC	AAA	27	3	0	0	4	4	24	25	3	3.0	9.0	24	43.7%	.324
2018	SF	MLB	27	10	10	0	28	26	145	153	19	3.4	7.0	112	42.9%	.308
2019	LAA	MLB	28	0	2	0	7	5	29¹	43	6	5.5	6.8	22	42.3%	.378
2019	PIT	MLB	28	1	1	0	28	0	46²	50	7	2.9	9.1	47	38.4%	.328
2020	PIT	MLB	29	2	1	0	27	0	30	26	3	3.9	11.7	39	48.1%	.303
2021 FS	PIT	MLB	30	2	2	7	57	0	50	46	7	3.4	8.9	49	43.0%	.293
2021 DC	PIT	MLB	30	2	2	7	57	0	61.3	57	9	3.4	8.9	60	43.0%	.293

Comparables: Sam Gaviglio, Kendall Graveman, Joe Kelly

In case you forgot from the comment above, the duo of Stratton-Rodríguez were worth more wins than the rest of the Pirates bullpen combined, so it's odd neither were moved at the trade deadline. Rodríguez has the more prototypical swing-and-miss stuff, but Stratton has a starter's complement of pitches with better underlying metrics, including elite spin on both his fastball and curve and an ability to generate lots of whiffs. In a perfect world, Stratton acts as a long reliever and Rodríguez is the setup man to Cederlind, but in another, more perfect world, both of them have been turned into prospects to further boost Pittsburgh's farm system.

YEAR	TEAM	LVL	AGE	WHIP	ERA	DRA-	WARP	MPH	FB%	WHF	CSP
2018	SAC	AAA	27	1.38	3.00	80	0.5				
2018	SF	MLB	27	1.43	5.09	111	0.5	92.6	62.2%	21.0%	
2019	LAA	MLB	28	2.08	8.59	185	-1.0	92.3	46.7%	22.7%	
2019	PIT	MLB	28	1.39	3.66	87	0.5	94.9	63.7%	25.6%	
2020	PIT	MLB	29	1.30	3.90	77	0.6	94.9	46.6%	35.3%	
2021 FS	PIT	MLB	30	1.32	4.14	93	0.4	93.9	56.3%	25.9%	47.0%
2021 DC	PIT	MLB	30	1.32	4.14	93	0.6	93.9	56.3%	25.9%	47.0%

Chris Stratton, continued

Pitch Shape vs LHH

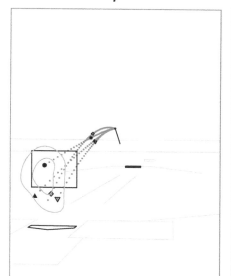

Pitch Shape vs RHH

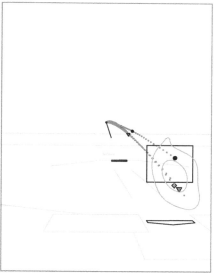

Type	Frequency	Velocity	H Movement	V Movement
● Fastball	46.3%	93.4 [103]	-3.8 [114]	-14.1 [103]
▲ Changeup	9.7%	86.5 [105]	-10.9 [104]	-27.8 [99]
▽ Slider	26.6%	87 [113]	4.7 [98]	-31.6 [106]
◇ Curveball	16.9%	80.3 [107]	14 [126]	-44.9 [108]

PLAYER COMMENTS WITHOUT GRAPHS

Anthony Alford   CF

Born: 07/20/94   Age: 26   Bats: R   Throws: R
Height: 6'1"   Weight: 210   Origin: Round 3, 2012 Draft (#112 overall)

YEAR	TEAM	LVL	AGE	PA	R	2B	3B	HR	RBI	BB	K	SB	CS	AVG/OBP/SLG
2018	DUN	HI-A	23	25	2	1	0	0	2	3	8	0	1	.200/.360/.250
2018	BUF	AAA	23	416	52	22	1	5	34	30	112	17	7	.240/.310/.344
2018	TOR	MLB	23	21	3	0	0	0	1	2	9	1	0	.105/.190/.105
2019	BUF	AAA	24	319	46	16	3	7	37	31	94	22	8	.259/.343/.411
2019	TOR	MLB	24	30	3	0	0	1	1	1	11	2	0	.179/.233/.286
2020	TOR	MLB	25	16	3	0	0	1	3	0	7	3	0	.188/.188/.375
2020	PIT	MLB	25	13	2	0	1	1	4	1	1	0	0	.250/.308/.667
2021 FS	PIT	MLB	26	600	62	23	1	15	57	48	195	12	5	.212/.288/.349
2021 DC	PIT	MLB	26	332	34	13	1	8	31	27	108	6	3	.212/.288/.349

Comparables: Clete Thomas, Drew Stubbs, Tyler Naquin

After being designated by Toronto, Alford's fresh start in Pittsburgh came to an abrupt halt in early September after an unfortunate tête-à-tête with the center-field wall in PNC Park. The good news is that he has history with both GM Ben Cherington and manager Derek Shelton, and the Pirates like his speed/defense combo as well as the potential pop in his bat. Alford runs the bases like a Rolls-Royce on a silk track, and when healthy will help a team with the second-fewest stolen bases in the NL in 2020.

YEAR	TEAM	LVL	AGE	PA	DRC+	BABIP	BRR	FRAA	WARP
2018	DUN	HI-A	23	25	72	.333	0.2	CF(2): -0.3, RF(2): -0.4, SS(1): 0.0	-0.1
2018	BUF	AAA	23	416	95	.327	4.5	CF(43): 2.9, LF(31): -1.7, RF(28): -1.0	0.8
2018	TOR	MLB	23	21	74	.200	0.7	LF(7): 0.2, RF(3): -0.1, CF(1): -0.0	0.1
2019	BUF	AAA	24	319	94	.365	1.4	RF(26): 3.8, CF(24): -4.4, LF(12): 1.4	0.8
2019	TOR	MLB	24	30	66	.250	0.3	LF(6): -0.3, RF(5): -0.0, CF(2): -0.1	0.0
2020	TOR	MLB	25	16	91	.250	0.4	LF(5): 0.0, CF(2): -0.4, RF(1): -0.0	0.0
2020	PIT	MLB	25	13	84	.200		CF(4): -0.5, LF(1): -0.2	-0.1
2021 FS	PIT	MLB	26	600	75	.301	0.6	RF 1, LF 0	-0.1
2021 DC	PIT	MLB	26	332	75	.301	0.3	RF 1, LF 0	-0.2

Will Craig 1B

Born: 11/16/94   Age: 26   Bats: R   Throws: R
Height: 6'3"   Weight: 220   Origin: Round 1, 2016 Draft (#22 overall)

YEAR	TEAM	LVL	AGE	PA	R	2B	3B	HR	RBI	BB	K	SB	CS	AVG/OBP/SLG
2018	ALT	AA	23	549	73	30	3	20	102	42	128	6	3	.248/.321/.448
2019	IND	AAA	24	556	69	23	0	23	78	44	146	2	3	.249/.326/.435
2020	PIT	MLB	25	4	0	0	0	0	0	0	1	0	0	.000/.000/.000
2021 FS	PIT	MLB	26	600	69	28	1	19	68	41	171	0	0	.232/.304/.399
2021 DC	PIT	MLB	26	145	16	6	0	4	16	10	41	0	0	.232/.304/.399

Comparables: Chad Santos, Brad Nelson, Bryan LaHair

When the Pirates called Craig up this year, he joined the great tradition of Pete Rose, Ernie Banks, and Stephen Drew, as players whose names are also sentences. Unlike those boldly declarative fellows, this Craig requires some interrogation: Will Craig hit? The 2016 first-rounder has shown an ability to hit for average and for power in pro ball, although never both at the same time. With Pittsburgh limited by the lack of the DH and both Bell and Moran blocking him at first, the more pressing question is not Will Craig, but Where Craig, and the answer seems to be a power-hungry AL team that won't mind his all-or-nothing approach in the box.

YEAR	TEAM	LVL	AGE	PA	DRC+	BABIP	BRR	FRAA	WARP
2018	ALT	AA	23	549	109	.288	0.6	1B(122): 8.8	1.3
2019	IND	AAA	24	556	94	.304	-0.4	1B(111): 0.7, RF(13): -1.1	0.2
2020	PIT	MLB	25	4	85	.000		1B(2): -0.1	0.0
2021 FS	PIT	MLB	26	600	92	.303	-0.9	1B 1, RF 0	0.2
2021 DC	PIT	MLB	26	145	92	.303	-0.2	1B 0	0.1

Oneil Cruz SS

Born: 10/04/98   Age: 22   Bats: L   Throws: R
Height: 6'7"   Weight: 215   Origin: International Free Agent, 2015

YEAR	TEAM	LVL	AGE	PA	R	2B	3B	HR	RBI	BB	K	SB	CS	AVG/OBP/SLG
2018	WV	LO-A	19	443	66	25	7	14	59	34	100	11	5	.286/.343/.488
2019	PIR	ROK	20	11	0	1	0	0	1	1	1	1	0	.600/.636/.700
2019	BRD	HI-A	20	145	21	6	1	7	16	8	38	7	3	.301/.345/.515
2019	ALT	AA	20	136	14	8	3	1	17	15	35	3	1	.269/.346/.412
2021 FS	PIT	MLB	22	600	63	26	7	14	63	41	208	7	4	.223/.282/.373
2021 DC	PIT	MLB	22	64	6	2	0	1	6	4	22	0	1	.223/.282/.373

Comparables: Nick Franklin, Jonathan Villar, Yu Chang

Nicknamed "la girafa" by his teammates, "la tarantula" might be more appropriate for a 6-foot-7 shortstop who seems to be all legs and arms. Scouts are divided on whether or not the lanky, limb-a-riffic Cruz will stick in the dirt or eventually move to the outfield, where his strong arm and easy plus power should play well in a corner. Cruz compensates for his XL levers by keeping his hands back and close to his body throughout his load before unleashing his bat in the zone like an abyssal tentacle. But the swing can get long at times and he's vulnerable to a pitcher attacking him inside. When he makes contact, however, the ball goes fast, and it goes far. An off-season auto accident in the Dominican Republic, where Cruz had returned to care for his pregnant girlfriend, clouds his future in baseball; prosecutors allege Cruz had alcohol in his system when his jeep struck a motorbike traveling without its lights, killing the driver and both passengers. If convicted, he could face anywhere from three to five years in prison. Even if he is acquitted of criminal negligence, he could face consequences for breaking the DR's strict curfew implemented to contain the spread of COVID-19 on the island.

YEAR	TEAM	LVL	AGE	PA	DRC+	BABIP	BRR	FRAA	WARP
2018	WV	LO-A	19	443	128	.346	2.5	SS(102): -5.9	2.1
2019	PIR	ROK	20	11		.667			
2019	BRD	HI-A	20	145	152	.374	0.1	SS(35): 2.2	1.6
2019	ALT	AA	20	136	121	.365	1.1	SS(35): 2.9	1.3
2021 FS	PIT	MLB	22	600	72	.332	0.9	SS 2	0.0
2021 DC	PIT	MLB	22	64	72	.332	0.1	SS 0	0.0

Wilmer Difo 2B

Born: 04/02/92   Age: 29   Bats: S   Throws: R
Height: 5'11"   Weight: 200   Origin: International Free Agent, 2010

YEAR	TEAM	LVL	AGE	PA	R	2B	3B	HR	RBI	BB	K	SB	CS	AVG/OBP/SLG
2018	WAS	MLB	26	456	55	14	7	7	42	39	82	10	3	.230/.298/.350
2019	FRE	AAA	27	261	48	14	3	4	30	25	51	13	5	.300/.369/.438
2019	WAS	MLB	27	144	15	2	0	2	8	12	29	0	1	.252/.315/.313
2020	WAS	MLB	28	18	1	0	0	0	1	3	4	0	0	.071/.222/.071
2021 FS	PIT	MLB	29	600	55	24	3	11	58	45	135	12	6	.233/.296/.352

Comparables: Emilio Bonifácio, Tony Womack, Bobby Knoop

Handed the keys to the second base job in 2018 after Daniel Murphy's departure, Difo promptly drove the car into a ditch, then spent the next season futilely trying to reverse out of it. For 2020, he didn't even bother getting behind the wheel, collecting a single hit in 18 plate appearances and getting designated for assignment in early September. Bereft of power and merely average defensively, Difo's career now has the trajectory of "light-hitting utility infielder," a kind of player that fell out of vogue years ago (though Tony La Russa is probably barking at someone to get Difo as you read this). That all doesn't bode well for him getting back into the driver's seat, or even squeezing into the middle seat in the back.

YEAR	TEAM	LVL	AGE	PA	DRC+	BABIP	BRR	FRAA	WARP
2018	WAS	MLB	26	456	78	.269	-1.5	2B(112): 4.7, 3B(20): -0.8, SS(9): 0.8	0.6
2019	FRE	AAA	27	261	94	.369	3.7	SS(32): -1.9, 2B(20): 1.4, 3B(10): -0.0	1.2
2019	WAS	MLB	27	144	74	.310	1.0	SS(33): -1.5, 3B(6): -0.3, 2B(2): 0.1	0.1
2020	WAS	MLB	28	18	96	.091	0.2	2B(4): -0.1, SS(4): -0.2, 3B(2): -0.0	0.0
2021 FS	PIT	MLB	29	600	79	.288	0.8	2B 2, SS -1	0.3

Nick Gonzales SS

Born: 05/27/99   Age: 22   Bats: R   Throws: R
Height: 5'10"   Weight: 190   Origin: Round 1, 2020 Draft (#7 overall)

A smaller stature and a lack of prospect pedigree held up some teams on Gonzales, so the Pirates were able to pounce on one of the draft's best pure hitters with the seventh pick. Shortly after signing, Pittsburgh sent him to the alternate training site, where he reportedly made hard contact against more advanced pitchers and earned praise from coaches for his mature approach on and off the field. A walk-on in college, Gonzales' work ethic compares favorably to legendary workhorse Alex Bregman, as does his short, powerful swing and lightning-quick hands. If not for the pandemic, he'd likely have shared Bregman's fast track to the majors; Gonzales swings an "angry bat," as one Pirates coach described it.

Mason Martin 1B

Born: 06/02/99   Age: 22   Bats: L   Throws: R
Height: 6'0"   Weight: 201   Origin: Round 17, 2017 Draft (#508 overall)

YEAR	TEAM	LVL	AGE	PA	R	2B	3B	HR	RBI	BB	K	SB	CS	AVG/OBP/SLG
2018	BRS	ROK	19	269	42	10	1	10	40	42	87	2	2	.233/.357/.422
2018	WV	LO-A	19	173	16	8	0	4	18	18	62	1	1	.200/.302/.333
2019	GBO	LO-A	20	355	58	19	3	23	83	46	103	8	2	.262/.361/.575
2019	BRD	HI-A	20	201	32	13	1	12	46	22	65	0	1	.239/.333/.528
2021 FS	PIT	MLB	22	600	50	20	2	12	53	56	241	2	1	.173/.257/.291

Comparables: Bobby Bradley, Chris Carter, Tyler O'Neill

A 17th-rounder who has never cracked a Top 100 list, the Pirates are nonetheless high on Martin, who earned their Minor League Player of the Year Award in 2019. With his bodybuilder father, Martin spent lockdown building strength, trimming his body fat towards the single digits, and gaining more flexibility to increase his swing speed. There is significant concern over the strikeout rate, especially as he enters the upper minors, but Martin knows how to take his walks, and the power is of the true light-tower variety, even if they have to widen the doors at Pirate City in order to admit his enormous biceps.

YEAR	TEAM	LVL	AGE	PA	DRC+	BABIP	BRR	FRAA	WARP
2018	BRS	ROK	19	269		.328			
2018	WV	LO-A	19	173	82	.310	0.0	1B(43): -3.0	-0.8
2019	GBO	LO-A	20	355	163	.311	-1.5	1B(77): 4.1	2.9
2019	BRD	HI-A	20	201	129	.303	-0.8	1B(47): 3.4	1.1
2021 FS	PIT	MLB	22	600	51	.283	-0.3	1B 2	-2.8

John Ryan Murphy C

Born: 05/13/91   Age: 30   Bats: R   Throws: R
Height: 5'11"   Weight: 200   Origin: Round 2, 2009 Draft (#76 overall)

YEAR	TEAM	LVL	AGE	PA	R	2B	3B	HR	RBI	BB	K	SB	CS	AVG/OBP/SLG
2018	ARI	MLB	27	223	19	9	0	9	24	11	71	0	0	.202/.244/.375
2019	GWN	AAA	28	50	5	0	0	1	3	2	13	0	0	.170/.220/.234
2019	RNO	AAA	28	136	26	7	0	9	26	12	34	0	0	.250/.316/.524
2019	ATL	MLB	28	1	0	0	0	0	0	0	0	0	0	.000/.000/.000
2019	ARI	MLB	28	69	9	3	0	4	7	6	28	0	0	.177/.250/.419
2020	PIT	MLB	29	63	6	2	0	0	2	4	28	0	0	.172/.226/.207
2021 FS	PIT	MLB	30	600	61	24	1	18	60	44	199	0	1	.198/.262/.347
2021 DC	PIT	MLB	30	58	5	2	0	1	5	4	19	0	0	.198/.262/.347

Comparables: Orlando McFarlane, Ron Karkovice, Austin Romine

Like that SNL skit about all moms having The Cut, all backup catchers have The Shag. JRM's fate was sealed when he showed up to summer camp with a thick crop of Gosewisch coming out of the back of his cap. The Pirates already have a somewhat light-hitting but Gold Glove-caliber defensive catcher in Stallings, so Murphy's

YEAR	TEAM	P. COUNT	FRM RUNS	BLK RUNS	THRW RUNS	TOT RUNS
2018	ARI	7638	9.3	0.3	-0.1	9.6
2019	ATL	31	0.0	0.0	0.0	0.0
2019	ARI	2433	0.0	1.3	0.0	1.3
2020	PIT	2713	0.7	-0.2	-0.1	0.4
2021	PIT	2405	1.2	0.0	0.1	1.3
2021	PIT	2405	1.2	0.0	0.1	1.3

presence on the roster is redundant. Fortunately for him, the Pirates' catching corps depth consists of a bag of shin guards, Michael Perez and a dartboard tied to an office chair.

YEAR	TEAM	LVL	AGE	PA	DRC+	BABIP	BRR	FRAA	WARP
2018	ARI	MLB	27	223	69	.256	-1.0	C(68): 10.2	1.2
2019	GWN	AAA	28	50	30	.212	0.1	C(14): 0.2	-0.1
2019	RNO	AAA	28	136	91	.272	1.4	C(31): -1.7	0.5
2019	ATL	MLB	28	1	142	.000		C(1): -0.0	0.0
2019	ARI	MLB	28	69	67	.233	0.3	C(18): 1.4, P(2): 0.0	0.2
2020	PIT	MLB	29	63	42	.333	-0.1	C(23): -0.0, P(1): -0.0	-0.3
2021 FS	PIT	MLB	30	600	63	.271	-0.9	C 11, 1B 0	0.6
2021 DC	PIT	MLB	30	58	63	.271	-0.1	C 1	0.1

Jared Oliva   CF

Born: 11/27/95   Age: 25   Bats: R   Throws: R
Height: 6'2"   Weight: 205   Origin: Round 7, 2017 Draft (#208 overall)

YEAR	TEAM	LVL	AGE	PA	R	2B	3B	HR	RBI	BB	K	SB	CS	AVG/OBP/SLG
2018	BRD	HI-A	22	454	75	24	4	9	47	40	91	33	8	.275/.354/.424
2019	ALT	AA	23	507	70	24	6	6	42	42	104	36	10	.277/.352/.398
2020	PIT	MLB	24	16	0	0	0	0	0	0	6	1	0	.188/.188/.188
2021 FS	PIT	MLB	25	600	60	28	5	12	59	41	179	21	7	.227/.292/.369
2021 DC	PIT	MLB	25	297	29	13	2	6	29	20	89	10	3	.227/.292/.369

Comparables: Daniel Fields, Tyler Naquin, Bryan Reynolds

It's hard not to root for Oliva, an overshadowed backup on his powerhouse prep team (Keston Hiura was among his teammates) and a walk-on at Arizona who blossomed after a stance change in his draft year. Oliva might not have the raw physical tools of a super-prospect, but he has the sixth tool of a high baseball IQ, constantly recording ideas and impressions in a notebook he carries into the dugout every game. Thanks to that feedback loop, Oliva is quick to make targeted adjustments when he struggles, without flailing around and losing the bedrock of his overall process. That ability to analyze, reflect and quickly correct course has propelled the 2017 seventh-rounder through Pittsburgh's system, leading to a debut at PNC Park in 2020. He likely profiles at worst as a speed-and-defense fourth outfielder, but one with enough on-base ability to compensate for below-average power.

YEAR	TEAM	LVL	AGE	PA	DRC+	BABIP	BRR	FRAA	WARP
2018	BRD	HI-A	22	454	126	.332	4.3	CF(101): -7.6	1.4
2019	ALT	AA	23	507	128	.347	4.2	CF(113): -1.2, LF(1): -0.1	3.4
2020	PIT	MLB	24	16	68	.300	0.0	LF(4): -0.7, CF(1): 0.1	-0.1
2021 FS	PIT	MLB	25	600	80	.315	2.1	LF -10, CF 1	-0.4
2021 DC	PIT	MLB	25	297	80	.315	1.1	LF -5, CF 0	-0.3

Liover Peguero SS

Born: 12/31/00   Age: 20   Bats: R   Throws: R
Height: 6'1"   Weight: 160   Origin: International Free Agent, 2017

YEAR	TEAM	LVL	AGE	PA	R	2B	3B	HR	RBI	BB	K	SB	CS	AVG/OBP/SLG
2018	DSL DB1	ROK	17	90	14	3	3	1	16	6	12	4	1	.309/.356/.457
2018	DIA	ROK	17	71	8	0	0	0	5	5	17	3	2	.197/.254/.197
2019	MIS	ROK+	18	156	34	7	3	5	27	12	34	8	1	.364/.410/.559
2019	HIL	SS	18	93	13	4	2	0	11	8	17	3	1	.262/.333/.357
2021 FS	PIT	MLB	20	600	45	22	6	7	50	30	188	11	4	.214/.257/.316

Comparables: Eduardo Núñez, Amed Rosario, Sergio Alcántara

Nailing (or failing) that first big trade is a crucial tone-setter for the duration of a new GM's tenure. It's too early to grade out the trade of Starling Marte for a pair of 19-year-olds in Peguero and hard-throwing righty Brennan Malone, but it certainly feels like the arrow is pointing in Pittsburgh's direction, even without the evidence of a minor-league season. Lean and long-legged, Peguero has a clean, balanced swing approach from the right side with plus bat speed and a good feel for the hitting zone. He should also continue to add power as he grows into his frame. On the dirt, he's a smooth and capable defender who projects to stick at short. Humble, enthusiastic, and deeply committed to his craft, the genial "Peggy" is a force in the clubhouse—he was a team leader on his NWL Championship Hillsboro Hops team—and likely a fan favorite in Pittsburgh for years to come, putting an early shine on that trade return.

YEAR	TEAM	LVL	AGE	PA	DRC+	BABIP	BRR	FRAA	WARP
2018	DSL DB1	ROK	17	90		.343			
2018	DIA	ROK	17	71		.265			
2019	MIS	ROK+	18	156		.448			
2019	HIL	SS	18	93	103	.328	0.1	SS(18): -0.1	0.4
2021 FS	PIT	MLB	20	600	55	.307	1.4	SS 4	-1.0

Travis Swaggerty   OF

Born: 08/19/97   Age: 23   Bats: L   Throws: L
Height: 5'11"   Weight: 180   Origin: Round 1, 2018 Draft (#10 overall)

YEAR	TEAM	LVL	AGE	PA	R	2B	3B	HR	RBI	BB	K	SB	CS	AVG/OBP/SLG
2018	WV	SS	20	158	22	9	1	4	15	15	40	9	3	.288/.365/.453
2018	WV	LO-A	20	71	6	1	1	1	5	7	18	0	0	.129/.225/.226
2019	BRD	HI-A	21	524	79	20	3	9	40	57	116	23	8	.265/.347/.381
2021 FS	PIT	MLB	23	600	52	22	3	12	57	43	191	9	4	.210/.272/.333

Comparables: Aaron Hicks, Jake Cave, Anthony Alford

The Pirates weren't put off by Swaggerty's poor performance after an aggressive promotion to full-season ball in his draft year. Instead they moved him up the ladder again to High-A, where he initially got off to a slow start but finished strong, with a .306/.375/.430 line in the second half. Swaggerty was ready to show that he's cleaned up the swing mechanics that led to many of his contact issues, but his coming-out party, and hopeful ascent to Top-100 lists, will have to wait. Even if he never taps into his raw over-the-fence power in games, there's an everyday centerfielder profile here, with good speed on the bases, a strong arm and solid defensive instincts, and an ability to take walks and get on base, provided the long layoff doesn't cost him the mechanical gains he made in 2019.

YEAR	TEAM	LVL	AGE	PA	DRC+	BABIP	BRR	FRAA	WARP
2018	WV	SS	20	158	146	.379	0.9	CF(36): -0.6	0.7
2018	WV	LO-A	20	71	43	.159	-0.6	CF(16): 0.7	-0.3
2019	BRD	HI-A	21	524	123	.334	-0.2	CF(121): 7.4	3.7
2021 FS	PIT	MLB	23	600	65	.297	0.6	CF 9	0.3

Tony Wolters   C

Born: 06/09/92   Age: 29   Bats: L   Throws: R
Height: 5'10"   Weight: 207   Origin: Round 3, 2010 Draft (#87 overall)

YEAR	TEAM	LVL	AGE	PA	R	2B	3B	HR	RBI	BB	K	SB	CS	AVG/OBP/SLG
2018	COL	MLB	26	216	19	4	4	3	27	26	32	2	0	.170/.292/.286
2019	COL	MLB	27	411	42	17	2	1	42	36	68	0	1	.262/.337/.329
2020	COL	MLB	28	109	10	4	0	0	8	6	30	0	0	.230/.280/.270
2021 FS	PIT	MLB	29	600	54	24	4	8	53	55	146	3	2	.223/.309/.335

Comparables: Duffy Dyer, Raul Casanova, John Rabb

Wolters hits like the ninth person in a lineup, which obviously wasn't commonplace in the Before Times version of the National League. But he was the last hitter in each of his 35 starts. It's not fair to say he hits like a pitcher, since 2019 NL hurlers OPSed .329 and he comfortably coasted past

YEAR	TEAM	P. COUNT	FRM RUNS	BLK RUNS	THRW RUNS	TOT RUNS
2018	COL	8013	10.2	-0.6	0.2	9.7
2019	COL	15067	-8.8	1.4	1.1	-6.4
2020	COL	4715	-2.3	-0.5	0.1	-2.8
2021	PIT	16650	4.7	-3.3	-0.7	0.6
2021	PIT	16650	4.7	-1.7	-0.7	2.2

that. But given that he's one of the league's weakest batters, and with his framing in decline, a more accurate (and brutal) way of putting it is that he hits and catches like a Wolters.

YEAR	TEAM	LVL	AGE	PA	DRC+	BABIP	BRR	FRAA	WARP
2018	COL	MLB	26	216	75	.188	2.5	C(64): 10.7, 2B(2): 0.0, LF(2): -0.0	1.8
2019	COL	MLB	27	411	84	.314	3.4	C(112): -4.5, 2B(8): -0.0, 3B(1): -0.0	1.2
2020	COL	MLB	28	109	63	.329	0.0	C(39): -0.7, 2B(4): -0.0	-0.5
2021 FS	PIT	MLB	29	600	77	.294	-0.1	C 2, 2B 0	0.9

Tyler Bashlor   RHP

Born: 04/16/93   Age: 28   Bats: R   Throws: R
Height: 6'0"   Weight: 195   Origin: Round 11, 2013 Draft (#326 overall)

YEAR	TEAM	LVL	AGE	W	L	SV	G	GS	IP	H	HR	BB/9	K/9	K	GB%	BABIP
2018	BNG	AA	25	0	3	7	20	0	24	14	2	4.5	11.2	30	26.4%	.245
2018	NYM	MLB	25	0	3	0	24	0	32	26	6	3.4	7.0	25	28.4%	.227
2019	SYR	AAA	26	3	2	8	33	0	37	29	3	3.6	9.0	37	34.0%	.277
2019	NYM	MLB	26	0	3	0	24	0	22	21	6	7.0	8.2	20	31.8%	.254
2020	PIT	MLB	27	0	0	0	8	0	8¹	9	2	4.3	6.5	6	46.2%	.292
2021 FS	PIT	MLB	28	2	2	0	57	0	50	46	8	4.0	9.1	50	35.0%	.286
2021 DC	PIT	MLB	28	1	1	0	25	0	27	25	4	4.0	9.1	27	35.0%	.286

Comparables: Michael Mariot, Yacksel Ríos, J.B. Wendelken

At the risk of invoking unfortunate comps, Bashlor does occasionally remind us that he has Great Stuff. The Joe Kelly parallels extend to his wavering control, but Kelly's pout game and even his moderately successful seasons remain as elusive to Bashlor as a well-located fastball.

YEAR	TEAM	LVL	AGE	WHIP	ERA	DRA-	WARP	MPH	FB%	WHF	CSP
2018	BNG	AA	25	1.08	2.62	67	0.5				
2018	NYM	MLB	25	1.19	4.22	126	-0.3	98.4	68.8%	24.4%	
2019	SYR	AAA	26	1.19	3.41	69	1.0				
2019	NYM	MLB	26	1.73	6.95	162	-0.6	97.9	62.2%	25.9%	
2020	PIT	MLB	27	1.56	8.64	108	0.0	97.5	48.9%	22.4%	
2021 FS	PIT	MLB	28	1.37	4.72	103	0.2	98.0	61.3%	24.6%	48.1%
2021 DC	PIT	MLB	28	1.37	4.72	103	0.1	98.0	61.3%	24.6%	48.1%

David Bednar   RHP

Born: 10/10/94   Age: 26   Bats: L   Throws: R
Height: 6'1"   Weight: 249   Origin: Round 35, 2016 Draft (#1044 overall)

YEAR	TEAM	LVL	AGE	W	L	SV	G	GS	IP	H	HR	BB/9	K/9	K	GB%	BABIP
2018	LE	HI-A	23	2	4	10	47	0	69^1	65	4	3.8	12.5	96	40.1%	.365
2019	AMA	AA	24	2	5	14	44	0	58	49	4	2.8	13.3	86	46.6%	.354
2019	SD	MLB	24	0	2	0	13	0	11	10	3	4.1	11.5	14	27.6%	.292
2020	SD	MLB	25	0	0	0	4	0	6^1	11	1	2.8	7.1	5	36.0%	.417
2021 FS	PIT	MLB	26	2	2	0	57	0	50	45	7	3.4	10.1	55	41.8%	.302
2021 DC	PIT	MLB	26	0	0	0	16	0	34	31	4	3.4	10.1	38	41.8%	.302

Comparables: Pedro Araujo, Matt Foster, Zac Reininger

Bednar relied more heavily on his fastball at the expense of his curve and splitter in 2020, but the only thing that improved was his walk rate. If he wants to be an effective middle reliever, he's going to need to miss more bats.

YEAR	TEAM	LVL	AGE	WHIP	ERA	DRA-	WARP	MPH	FB%	WHF	CSP
2018	LE	HI-A	23	1.36	2.73	75	1.0				
2019	AMA	AA	24	1.16	2.95	69	0.9				
2019	SD	MLB	24	1.36	6.55	92	0.1	96.5	43.4%	32.6%	
2020	SD	MLB	25	2.05	7.11	106	0.0	97.7	59.3%	27.7%	
2021 FS	PIT	MLB	26	1.30	4.11	93	0.4	97.0	50.9%	30.3%	51.0%
2021 DC	PIT	MLB	26	1.30	4.11	93	0.3	97.0	50.9%	30.3%	51.0%

Blake Cederlind   RHP

Born: 01/04/96   Age: 25   Bats: R   Throws: R
Height: 6'4"   Weight: 205   Origin: Round 5, 2016 Draft (#165 overall)

YEAR	TEAM	LVL	AGE	W	L	SV	G	GS	IP	H	HR	BB/9	K/9	K	GB%	BABIP
2018	WV	LO-A	22	3	2	1	19	1	28¹	21	1	2.9	11.4	36	50.0%	.312
2018	BRD	HI-A	22	1	2	3	17	0	21¹	26	2	8.0	7.6	18	58.0%	.358
2019	BRD	HI-A	23	0	0	2	7	0	7²	4	0	7.0	9.4	8	50.0%	.200
2019	ALT	AA	23	5	1	2	31	0	45²	31	1	3.2	8.3	42	48.8%	.252
2019	IND	AAA	23	0	1	0	3	0	6	11	1	3.0	7.5	5	52.0%	.435
2020	PIT	MLB	24	0	0	0	5	0	4	3	0	2.2	9.0	4	54.5%	.273
2021 FS	*PIT*	*MLB*	*25*	*2*	*3*	*0*	*57*	*0*	*50*	*48*	*7*	*5.5*	*8.2*	*45*	*45.9%*	*.295*
2021 DC	*PIT*	*MLB*	*25*	*1*	*1*	*0*	*25*	*0*	*27*	*26*	*3*	*5.5*	*8.2*	*24*	*45.9%*	*.295*

Comparables: Stephen Nogosek, José Ruiz, James Norwood

This past spring training Cederlind sported a glorious golden mane, which, combined with his tendency to stick out his tongue and widen his eyes mid-delivery, made it seem like a War Boy had slipped loose of Immortan Joe and was throwing triple-digit heat. (He also has a legit strikeout strut that would make Foghorn Leghorn envious.) He cut the hair before making his MLB debut, and more's the pity, but the stuff was plenty loud on its own; the first pitch he threw in MLB came in at 98 mph, and he'll regularly work 98-100, complemented with a slider at 90-92 that ties up hitters. As with any reliever with big big stuff, there's volatility present, but when he's on he shows flashes of being a top-tier closer, able to dot high-octane stuff around the zone like a War Boy wielding silver spray paint. Witness him!

YEAR	TEAM	LVL	AGE	WHIP	ERA	DRA-	WARP	MPH	FB%	WHF	CSP
2018	WV	LO-A	22	1.06	2.86	62	0.6				
2018	BRD	HI-A	22	2.11	7.59	135	-0.4				
2019	BRD	HI-A	23	1.30	1.17	77	0.1				
2019	ALT	AA	23	1.03	1.77	81	0.4				
2019	IND	AAA	23	2.17	7.50	166	-0.1				
2020	PIT	MLB	24	1.00	4.50	87	0.1	100.0	100.0%	32.1%	
2021 FS	*PIT*	*MLB*	*25*	*1.59*	*5.50*	*115*	*-0.2*	*100.0*	*100.0%*	*32.1%*	*53.3%*
2021 DC	*PIT*	*MLB*	*25*	*1.59*	*5.50*	*115*	*-0.1*	*100.0*	*100.0%*	*32.1%*	*53.3%*

Kyle Crick   RHP

Born: 11/30/92   Age: 28   Bats: L   Throws: R
Height: 6'4"   Weight: 225   Origin: Round 1, 2011 Draft (#49 overall)

YEAR	TEAM	LVL	AGE	W	L	SV	G	GS	IP	H	HR	BB/9	K/9	K	GB%	BABIP
2018	PIT	MLB	25	3	2	2	64	0	60¹	45	3	3.4	9.7	65	41.2%	.269
2019	PIT	MLB	26	3	7	0	52	0	49	41	10	6.4	11.2	61	41.5%	.274
2020	PIT	MLB	27	0	1	0	7	0	5²	7	0	6.4	11.1	7	33.3%	.389
2021 FS	PIT	MLB	28	2	2	5	57	0	50	42	5	5.5	10.2	56	39.9%	.294
2021 DC	PIT	MLB	28	2	2	5	57	0	61.3	52	7	5.5	10.2	69	39.9%	.294

Comparables: Phil Maton, Archie Bradley, John Curtiss

Crick's fastball velocity was down significantly, his slider lost about 250 RPM, and he had two different stints on the IL for a lat strain. But also, he enters arbitration for the first time this year making the minimum with only five innings pitched in 2020. "This wine is awful," declares Moira Rose/Ben Cherington. "Get me another glass."

YEAR	TEAM	LVL	AGE	WHIP	ERA	DRA-	WARP	MPH	FB%	WHF	CSP
2018	PIT	MLB	25	1.13	2.39	98	0.4	97.4	72.8%	27.4%	
2019	PIT	MLB	26	1.55	4.96	114	-0.1	96.5	62.3%	29.6%	
2020	PIT	MLB	27	1.94	1.59	97	0.1	92.5	45.2%	31.8%	
2021 FS	PIT	MLB	28	1.46	4.54	97	0.3	96.4	63.9%	29.1%	46.4%
2021 DC	PIT	MLB	28	1.46	4.54	97	0.4	96.4	63.9%	29.1%	46.4%

Wil Crowe RHP

Born: 09/09/94   Age: 26   Bats: R   Throws: R
Height: 6'2"   Weight: 228   Origin: Round 2, 2017 Draft (#65 overall)

YEAR	TEAM	LVL	AGE	W	L	SV	G	GS	IP	H	HR	BB/9	K/9	K	GB%	BABIP
2018	AUB	SS	23	0	0	0	1	1	3	2	0	6.0	3.0	1	62.5%	.250
2018	FBG	HI-A	23	11	0	0	16	15	87	71	6	3.1	8.1	78	45.8%	.270
2018	HBG	AA	23	0	5	0	5	5	26¹	31	4	5.5	5.1	15	42.5%	.325
2019	HBG	AA	24	7	6	0	16	16	95¹	85	8	2.1	8.4	89	48.1%	.297
2019	FRE	AAA	24	0	4	0	10	10	54	66	7	4.3	6.8	41	41.2%	.337
2020	WAS	MLB	25	0	2	0	3	3	8¹	14	5	8.6	8.6	8	27.6%	.375
2021 FS	PIT	MLB	26	8	9	0	26	26	150	154	27	4.4	7.3	121	40.4%	.291
2021 DC	PIT	MLB	26	3	4	0	12	12	59.3	61	10	4.4	7.3	48	40.4%	.291

Comparables: Mitch White, Brady Lail, Joel Payamps

MLB debuts are supposed to be happy moments, but Crowe will probably want to forget every inning of his brief stay at the top in 2020. The former second-round pick got a shot as a fill-in starter for a trio of doubleheaders late in the season and was bombed from orbit in all three, failing to make it past the fourth inning each time. Crowe, a mid-rotation prospect thanks to a hard fastball and a mix of average or better secondary offerings, was moved to the Pirates in the Josh Bell trade, meaning he'll get a fresh start to help him forget the misery that was his first go at the big leagues.

YEAR	TEAM	LVL	AGE	WHIP	ERA	DRA-	WARP	MPH	FB%	WHF	CSP
2018	AUB	SS	23	1.33	0.00	106	0.0				
2018	FBG	HI-A	23	1.16	2.69	71	2.0				
2018	HBG	AA	23	1.78	6.15	100	0.2				
2019	HBG	AA	24	1.12	3.87	92	0.5				
2019	FRE	AAA	24	1.70	6.17	126	0.3				
2020	WAS	MLB	25	2.64	11.88	180	-0.3	93.2	57.2%	19.4%	
2021 FS	PIT	MLB	26	1.52	5.46	117	0.0	93.2	57.2%	19.4%	40.9%
2021 DC	PIT	MLB	26	1.52	5.46	117	0.0	93.2	57.2%	19.4%	40.9%

Michael Feliz   RHP

Born: 06/28/93   Age: 28   Bats: R   Throws: R
Height: 6'4"   Weight: 240   Origin: International Free Agent, 2010

YEAR	TEAM	LVL	AGE	W	L	SV	G	GS	IP	H	HR	BB/9	K/9	K	GB%	BABIP
2018	IND	AAA	25	2	1	2	9	0	10	13	2	0.9	10.8	12	40.0%	.393
2018	PIT	MLB	25	1	2	0	47	0	47²	49	6	4.3	10.4	55	33.1%	.331
2019	IND	AAA	26	0	0	2	10	0	15	13	1	4.2	13.2	22	34.3%	.364
2019	PIT	MLB	26	4	4	0	58	1	56¹	44	11	4.3	11.7	73	35.8%	.264
2020	PIT	MLB	27	0	0	0	3	0	1²	4	1	10.8	10.8	2	28.6%	.500
2021 FS	PIT	MLB	28	2	2	1	57	0	50	41	7	4.4	10.9	60	35.7%	.287
2021 DC	PIT	MLB	28	2	2	1	57	0	61.3	51	9	4.4	10.9	74	35.7%	.287

Comparables: Keone Kela, Phil Maton, Dan Altavilla

Early 2000s Canadian indie rock band Hot Hot Heat had one driving mandate: to create abnormally catchy post-punk pop songs. With a similarly fixed mindset, Astros pitching development (Deliz arrived from Houston in the Gerrit Cole trade) prides the almighty strikeout and Hot Hot Heat, without worrying so much about limiting walks. Elite velocity can prop up that approach, but Feliz's fastball is more mid-90s than high-90s, and poor command means he falls behind in counts and cannot effectively access his putaway weapon in the slider, resulting in walks or poorly-located fastballs that get punished. A forearm strain wiped out most of his 2020 season, and might have been the reason he'd lost a full tick off his fastball. As it turns out, relying entirely on frenetically-paced earworms with no clear direction isn't a sustainable way to build an enduring musical career, nor a late-innings reliever.

YEAR	TEAM	LVL	AGE	WHIP	ERA	DRA-	WARP	MPH	FB%	WHF	CSP
2018	IND	AAA	25	1.40	7.20	50	0.3				
2018	PIT	MLB	25	1.51	5.66	116	-0.1	97.0	73.6%	24.3%	
2019	IND	AAA	26	1.33	1.20	63	0.5				
2019	PIT	MLB	26	1.26	3.99	69	1.2	97.5	73.4%	29.0%	
2020	PIT	MLB	27	3.60	32.40	91	0.0	96.2	55.0%	27.8%	
2021 FS	PIT	MLB	28	1.32	4.07	91	0.5	97.3	72.4%	27.5%	45.9%
2021 DC	PIT	MLB	28	1.32	4.07	91	0.6	97.3	72.4%	27.5%	45.9%

Jared Jones   RHP
Born: 08/06/01   Age: 19   Bats: L   Throws: R
Height: 6'1"   Weight: 180   Origin: Round 2, 2020 Draft (#44 overall)

Jones tantalized scouts as a prep talent with a right arm capable of launching balls at warp speeds from the outfield, but most scouts believe the two-way prospect's future is on the mound, where his exceptional arm speed manifests in a tailing fastball that kisses triple digits. A high-effort, short-armed overhand delivery and bulldog mentality on the mound seem to telegraph a future bullpen role as a high-leverage reliever, especially as his second-best pitch currently is a swing-and-miss slider that mostly just lacks consistency. The Pirates have him working on a changeup and a curve and will give their second-rounder every opportunity to start, but a fast track to The Show as a power reliever feels like the likelier outcome.

Keone Kela   RHP
Born: 04/16/93   Age: 28   Bats: R   Throws: R
Height: 6'1"   Weight: 220   Origin: Round 12, 2012 Draft (#396 overall)

YEAR	TEAM	LVL	AGE	W	L	SV	G	GS	IP	H	HR	BB/9	K/9	K	GB%	BABIP
2018	TEX	MLB	25	3	3	24	38	0	36²	28	3	3.4	10.8	44	39.4%	.278
2018	PIT	MLB	25	0	1	0	16	0	15¹	10	2	2.9	12.9	22	27.3%	.258
2019	PIT	MLB	26	2	0	1	32	0	29²	19	3	3.3	10.0	33	36.5%	.225
2020	PIT	MLB	27	0	0	0	3	0	2	3	1	4.5	13.5	3	50.0%	.400
2021 FS	PIT	MLB	28	2	2	0	57	0	50	39	6	4.4	11.5	63	38.5%	.279
2021 DC	PIT	MLB	28	2	2	0	47	0	41	32	5	4.4	11.5	52	38.5%	.279

Comparables: Dominic Leone, Dan Altavilla, Phil Maton

Part of Pittsburgh's failure to add to their farm system at the trade deadline wasn't their fault, as their main piece of trade bait wound up bitten by the injury bug. A positive COVID test kept Kela out until August, and when he did return, a forearm strain polished off what remained of his Pirates career. Given his talent, a contending team seeking back-end bullpen help should snatch the hard-throwing righty up; given his health, temperament, and the state of the market, they might not.

YEAR	TEAM	LVL	AGE	WHIP	ERA	DRA-	WARP	MPH	FB%	WHF	CSP
2018	TEX	MLB	25	1.15	3.44	78	0.6	98.5	64.3%	29.4%	
2018	PIT	MLB	25	0.98	2.93	53	0.5	98.3	58.7%	35.2%	
2019	PIT	MLB	26	1.01	2.12	78	0.5	98.2	53.5%	27.1%	
2020	PIT	MLB	27	2.00	4.50	86	0.0	97.7	48.1%	26.9%	
2021 FS	PIT	MLB	28	1.27	3.52	83	0.7	98.3	57.0%	28.7%	47.6%
2021 DC	PIT	MLB	28	1.27	3.52	83	0.6	98.3	57.0%	28.7%	47.6%

Mike Loree   RHP

Born: 09/14/86   Age: 34   Bats: R   Throws: R
Height: 6'6"   Weight: 226   Origin: Round 50, 2007 Draft (#1441 overall)

YEAR	TEAM	LVL	AGE	W	L	SV	G	GS	IP	H	HR	BB/9	K/9	K	GB%	BABIP
2018	FUB	CPBL	31	10	8	0	26	26	161	177	15	0.9	8.8	157		
2019	FUB	CPBL	32	13	10	0	28	28	179^2	149	13	1.7	8.7	173		
2020	FUB	CPBL	33	6	12	0	25	25	144^2	186	16	1.9	8.5	136		
2021									No projection							

In a league where foreign players rarely stick around for too long, Loree is an exception. Save for a pitstop in Korea in 2014, he's been a stalwart of the CPBL since 2012, making 2020 his eighth season in the league–the most for a foreign pitcher since the Domincan-born Osvaldo Martinez from 1997-2005. And it's not just his service time that makes him stand out, as Loree has consistently ranked among the best starters in the league for the better half of the past decade. Never a particularly hard thrower, Loree commands his tailing high-80s fastball impeccably, and CPBL batters are still baffled by his splitter. When it's all said and done for Loree–under contract to return to Fubon in 2021–he'll undoubtedly be viewed as one of the most accomplished pitchers in the league's history.

YEAR	TEAM	LVL	AGE	WHIP	ERA	DRA-	WARP	MPH	FB%	WHF	CSP
2018	FUB	CPBL	31	1.20	3.47						
2019	FUB	CPBL	32	1.02	2.76						
2020	FUB	CPBL	33	1.49	5.23						
2021					No projection						

Brennan Malone   RHP

Born: 09/08/00   Age: 20   Bats: R   Throws: R
Height: 6'4"   Weight: 205   Origin: Round 1, 2019 Draft (#33 overall)

YEAR	TEAM	LVL	AGE	W	L	SV	G	GS	IP	H	HR	BB/9	K/9	K	GB%	BABIP
2019	DIA	ROK	18	1	2	0	6	3	7	4	0	6.4	9.0	7	33.3%	.222
2019	HIL	SS	18	0	0	0	1	0	1	0	0	0.0	9.0	1	50.0%	.000
2021 FS	PIT	MLB	20	2	3	0	57	0	50	49	8	6.5	7.8	43	35.9%	.285

Comparables: Elvis Luciano, Devin Williams, Randy Rosario

It's hard to overlook a 6'4" chunk of rock face like Malone's. But through a combination of factors—he threw only eight innings as a pro before being shipped to the no-frills Steel City, lifting weights in his North Carolina driveway through most of the COVID-shortened season—even die-hard yinzers might not know the gem-in-waiting they have in Malone, who is built to factory specs for a frontline starter. A thrower more than a pitcher in high school, Malone is learning to harness his elite velocity while working on sharpening his occasionally-loopy curveball and changeup. A late-breaking slider with tight spin remains his best out pitch and can give righties fits. If the Pirates go chalk and select Vanderbilt's Kumar Rocker first overall in the 2021 draft, the potential one-two punch of Rocker and Malone could drive twin road graders over NL Central lineups for years to come, years from now.

YEAR	TEAM	LVL	AGE	WHIP	ERA	DRA-	WARP	MPH	FB%	WHF	CSP
2019	DIA	ROK	18	1.29	5.14						
2019	HIL	SS	18	0.00	0.00	68	0.0				
2021 FS	PIT	MLB	20	1.70	5.97	127	-0.5				

Carmen Mlodzinski   RHP

Born: 02/19/99   Age: 22   Bats: R   Throws: R
Height: 6'2"   Weight: 232   Origin: Round 1, 2020 Draft (#31 overall)

Pronounced "Ma-jin-ski," the former Gamecock was snatched up by the Pirates with the 31st-overall pick in the 2020 draft despite limited looks, thanks largely to a strong performance on the Cape where he showcased swing-and-miss stuff on a mid-90s fastball and a hard slider/curveball. That alone gives him a safe floor in the bullpen, but he also throws a cutter and a solid changeup, all with plus command, that give him solid middle-of-the-rotation potential. With an abbreviated college track record and absolutely no social media where fans can follow his journey, Mlodzinski will continue working, building a mlodzystery, and choosing his pitches carefully.

Quinn Priester   RHP

Born: 09/15/00   Age: 20   Bats: R   Throws: R
Height: 6'3"   Weight: 195   Origin: Round 1, 2019 Draft (#18 overall)

YEAR	TEAM	LVL	AGE	W	L	SV	G	GS	IP	H	HR	BB/9	K/9	K	GB%	BABIP
2019	PIR	ROK	18	1	1	0	8	7	32²	29	1	2.8	10.2	37	57.3%	.322
2019	WV	SS	18	0	0	0	1	1	4	3	0	9.0	9.0	4	90.0%	.300
2021 FS	PIT	MLB	20	2	3	0	57	0	50	48	8	5.3	8.0	44	47.9%	.286

Comparables: Junior Fernández, Brad Keller, Ronald Herrera

Priester was the last first-rounder selected by the previous regime and surprise, surprise, he throws a sinker. But he also throws a gorgeous 12-6 curveball that was among the best in his draft class and commands his pitches well, with clean mechanics and more polish than is typical for a cold-weather prep prospect. The 19-year-old was summoned to join the player pool at Altoona when Ke'Bryan Hayes was called up, and was reportedly sitting 96-97, touching 98, with his fastball this summer. He's also working on a changeup that was undeveloped, probably because unlike other top pitching prospects he didn't have a pitching coach until joining the Pirates organization. Prior to being called to the player pool, Priester made an impression with Pirates fans this summer when the Cary, IL native and erstwhile Cubs fan joined his mother to cheer on his new team from a Wrigleyville rooftop—a place he visited often with his grandfather, whom he had lost to COVID-19 just months earlier. It is an undeniable tragedy John Foley will never be able to watch his grandson pitch from those same bleachers, but what a special moment it will be when Priester makes his debut at Wrigley Field. Book your rooftop seat now.

YEAR	TEAM	LVL	AGE	WHIP	ERA	DRA-	WARP	MPH	FB%	WHF	CSP
2019	PIR	ROK	18	1.19	3.03						
2019	WV	SS	18	1.75	4.50	100	0.0				
2021 FS	PIT	MLB	20	1.56	5.43	119	-0.3				

José Soriano   RHP

Born: 10/20/98   Age: 22   Bats: R   Throws: R
Height: 6'3"   Weight: 220   Origin: International Free Agent, 2016

YEAR	TEAM	LVL	AGE	W	L	SV	G	GS	IP	H	HR	BB/9	K/9	K	GB%	BABIP
2018	BUR	LO-A	19	1	6	0	14	14	46¹	34	1	6.8	8.2	42	45.3%	.284
2019	ANG	ROK	20	0	1	0	3	3	4²	5	0	5.8	15.4	8	25.0%	.417
2019	BUR	LO-A	20	5	6	0	17	15	77²	53	5	5.6	9.7	84	54.0%	.262
2021 FS	PIT	MLB	22	2	3	0	57	0	50	47	7	6.4	8.2	45	44.2%	.285
2021 DC	PIT	MLB	22	2	2	0	22	3	33.3	31	5	6.4	8.2	30	44.2%	.285

Comparables: Chris Flexen, Alex Reyes, Huascar Ynoa

Going under the knife is rarely fortuitous, especially in the case of Tommy John surgery. Still, getting TJ a month before the world ended and took the minor-league season with it—as Soriano did in February—counts as pretty solid timing. The Pirates still took him with the top pick in the Rule 5 Draft, and while he's likely to be sidelined into 2021, his mid-90s velocity gives him a chance to stick in a relief role once he heals.

YEAR	TEAM	LVL	AGE	WHIP	ERA	DRA-	WARP	MPH	FB%	WHF	CSP
2018	BUR	LO-A	19	1.49	4.47	89	0.6				
2019	ANG	ROK	20	1.71	1.93						
2019	BUR	LO-A	20	1.30	2.55	90	0.7				
2021 FS	PIT	MLB	22	1.66	5.70	120	-0.3				
2021 DC	PIT	MLB	22	1.66	5.70	120	-0.2				

Wei-Chung Wang   LHP

Born: 04/25/92   Age: 29   Bats: L   Throws: L
Height: 6'1"   Weight: 160   Origin: International Free Agent, 2011

YEAR	TEAM	LVL	AGE	W	L	SV	G	GS	IP	H	HR	BB/9	K/9	K	GB%	BABIP
2019	LV	AAA	27	1	1	1	19	0	26¹	29	5	2.7	8.2	24	43.4%	.316
2019	OAK	MLB	27	1	0	0	20	0	27	22	4	3.7	5.3	16	30.5%	.231
2019	PIT	MLB	27	2	0	0	5	0	4	5	0	6.8	4.5	2	64.3%	.357
2021 FS	PIT	MLB	29	2	2	0	57	0	50	46	7	3.4	7.3	40	40.4%	.274

Comparables: Tyler Duffey, Brooks Pounders, Cory Mazzoni

The Dragons are joining the CPBL for the 2021 season, and their biggest splash to date was bringing aboard Wang, a recent big-leaguer who became a clear choice as the first pick of the 2020 CPBL draft after announcing his return to Taiwan. Following a few months of negotiation, the Dragons ultimately lured Wang with the most lucrative contract in the CPBL's history (a five-year deal worth slightly over $2 million USD). Wang and his four-pitch mix will still be just 28 at the start of the season, and stands to be the Dragons' clear-cut ace.

YEAR	TEAM	LVL	AGE	WHIP	ERA	DRA-	WARP	MPH	FB%	WHF	CSP
2019	LV	AAA	27	1.41	4.78	76	0.6				
2019	OAK	MLB	27	1.22	3.33	151	-0.6	94.0	43.1%	21.7%	
2019	PIT	MLB	27	2.00	6.75	44	0.1	93.9	47.4%	11.4%	
2021 FS	PIT	MLB	29	1.31	4.16	95	0.4	94.0	43.7%	20.2%	46.5%

Miguel Yajure   RHP

Born: 05/01/98   Age: 23   Bats: R   Throws: R
Height: 6'1"   Weight: 175   Origin: International Free Agent, 2015

YEAR	TEAM	LVL	AGE	W	L	SV	G	GS	IP	H	HR	BB/9	K/9	K	GB%	BABIP
2018	CSC	LO-A	20	4	3	0	14	14	64²	64	3	2.1	7.8	56	50.3%	.316
2019	TAM	HI-A	21	8	6	0	22	18	127²	110	5	2.0	8.6	122	54.8%	.301
2019	TRN	AA	21	1	0	0	2	2	11	9	0	1.6	9.0	11	35.5%	.290
2020	NYY	MLB	22	0	0	0	3	0	7	3	1	6.4	10.3	8	40.0%	.143
2021 FS	PIT	MLB	23	2	3	0	57	0	50	50	9	3.4	7.8	43	38.2%	.294
2021 DC	PIT	MLB	23	3	3	0	34	6	40.7	41	7	3.4	7.8	35	38.2%	.294

Comparables: Jonathan Hernández, Rony García, Zack Littell

Yajure impressed in his major-league debut despite reduced velocity from the year prior. Like many Yankee pitching prospects pressed into service in 2020, he needs more minor-league reps. Should all go well—and it seldom does, in baseball or life—he could become a back-end starter.

YEAR	TEAM	LVL	AGE	WHIP	ERA	DRA-	WARP	MPH	FB%	WHF	CSP
2018	CSC	LO-A	20	1.22	3.90	104	0.2				
2019	TAM	HI-A	21	1.08	2.26	78	1.8				
2019	TRN	AA	21	1.00	0.82	104	0.0				
2020	NYY	MLB	22	1.14	1.29	93	0.1	93.9	50.0%	22.0%	
2021 FS	PIT	MLB	23	1.40	4.94	108	0.0	93.9	50.0%	22.0%	43.5%
2021 DC	PIT	MLB	23	1.40	4.94	108	0.0	93.9	50.0%	22.0%	43.5%

Yao-Hsun Yang 陽耀勳　LHP

Born: 01/22/83　Age: 38　Bats: L　Throws: L
Height: 5'11"　Weight: 210　Origin:

YEAR	TEAM	LVL	AGE	W	L	SV	G	GS	IP	H	HR	BB/9	K/9	K	GB%	BABIP
2019	LAM	CPBL	36	0	0	0	1	0	1²	2	0	10.8	10.8	2		
2020	RAK	CPBL	37	0	0	0	1	0	1	1	0	9.0	18.0	2		
2021									No projection							

At 38 years of age, Yang's professional playing career could be described as a play in three acts. Debuting in 2006, The Taitung native pitched for the NPB's Fukuoka Softbank Hawks until 2013, peaking with a stretch between 2010 and 2012 where he pitched to a 1.79 ERA across 75 ⅓ innings. The second act in this play was a brief one: a stint in affiliated ball after signing with the Pittsburgh Pirates in 2014. He pitched 16⅔ unspectacular innings for Double-A Altoona before his release that July. The third act is still being written–Yang returned to his home country to play for the Monkeys in 2015, but this time around, he decided to forgo pitching and convert to outfield duty full-time. These last-ditch efforts are rarely successful, but Yang is proof that rarely doesn't mean never. Despite being one of the older players in the league, he's coming off his finest season since 2017.

YEAR	TEAM	LVL	AGE	WHIP	ERA	DRA-	WARP	MPH	FB%	WHF	CSP
2019	LAM	CPBL	36	2.40	5.40						
2020	RAK	CPBL	37	2.00	0.00						
2021						No projection					

Pirates Prospects

The State of the System:

There's plenty of high upside talent in the Pirates' system now, but this rebuild is probably going to last a while longer given the lack of overall depth.

The Top Ten:

─────── ★ ★ ★ *2021 Top 101 Prospect* **#7** ★ ★ ★ ───────

1 | **Ke'Bryan Hayes** **3B**   OFP: 70   ETA: Debuted in 2020
Born: 01/28/97   Age: 24   Bats: R   Throws: R   Height: 5'10"   Weight: 205
Origin: Round 1, 2015 Draft (#32 overall)

The Report: If you got to the park by 4 p.m., Hayes looked like a perennial All-Star in waiting. He'd flash plus-plus raw power at the end of batting practice, and early on when he was taking it easy and getting loose, would still crack laser beam line drives from gap to gap. The plus-or-better glove at third base was obvious as well. At 7 p.m.? Well, he still looked like a very good third base prospect. The glove was more obviously plus-plus as he'd slow the game down, or fire an accurate strike from a step or two into foul territory. There was a strong approach at the plate, and he'd hit the ball incredibly hard—it's at least 70-grade bat speed. But Hayes didn't lift pitches consistently, instead ripping doubles down the left field line when he really got into one. He never managed double-digit home run totals until 2019 with the Triple-A rabbit ball, in what was overall a bit of a disappointing campaign. The lack of game power seemed to limit the upside to merely a good regular as Hayes stood on the precipice of the majors.

Development Track: After implying that Hayes could have the everyday third base job if he just signed a cheap extension, the Pirates finally gave him some run at the hot corner at the end of a lost season. If you want a bright spot for the 2020 season—in addition to securing the first overall pick, I guess—he immediately found that missing over-the-fence game power. And these home runs weren't cheapies. It's not a large enough sample size to be sure it will play as plus going forward—he's still list eligible, after all—but it looked very, very right. As did the rest of the offensive profile and the glove at third. But we've long been pretty sure about those.

Variance: Medium. Hayes was always likely to be a good regular given the approach, plus hit tool, and plus-plus glove. How real the 2020 power breakout is will dictate exactly how good a regular.

Mark Barry's Fantasy Take: I long loved Hayes, believing his minor-league numbers masked his true upside. Then around this time last year, I hedged like a coward and tempered expectations as to whether Hayes could be an impact bat. Yes, it's fewer than 100 plate appearances, but Hayes looks every bit like That Dude, making a ton of loud contact and finding a way to consistently leave the yard. Hayes is a top-10 dynasty name, for me, pushing top five, and I'm sorry for doubting him.

─────── ★ ★ ★ *2021 Top 101 Prospect* **#39** ★ ★ ★ ───────

2

Nick Gonzales SS   OFP: 60   ETA: 2023
Born: 05/27/99   Age: 22   Bats: R   Throws: R   Height: 5'10"   Weight: 190
Origin: Round 1, 2020 Draft (#7 overall)

The Report: This is not your typical top-of-the-draft, top-of-the-system prospect. Undersized, from a smaller school, playing a non-premium position, Gonzales somehow managed to win over the detractors to the point where his selection didn't even merit the bat of an eye. Look past the video game numbers racked up at the friendly confines of New Mexico State's extreme hitter's park and toward the campaign he put up at the Cape Cod League. As the 2019 MVP he slashed .351/.451/.630 against consistently better competition and in a pitcher's league. The swing is lightning quick with excellent hand-speed, angling his torso at the waist to create tons of natural lift. He may get a few looks at other positions, second base seems like the most likely fit where his offense would play up comparatively against his peers.

Development Track: Consider this next part as an extension of his report, but one attribute that might be his best tool is his makeup. One scout at the Cape likened him to Bryce Harper as the quintessential gym rat, constantly working out and trying to improve his game. While at school, he even reportedly was giving switch-hitting a try in the batting cages. All this to impress upon the point that even though his defense may be lacking, it's not because of any lack of effort. He's known to flash a stellar play a time or two, what he needs is more consistency and concentration in the field with his physical ability taking over.

Variance: Medium. Borderline low variance, but still needs to adjust to quality pitching day-in, day-out. Knowing how much he'll likely work his tail off, it helps quell most fear associated with his future.

Mark Barry's Fantasy Take: There are a couple of questions re: Gonzales from a fantasy standpoint: 1) How real was the power in such a power-friendly environment like New Mexico? and 2) Will he run at all? I think he'll make a ton of contact, but it might not be fantasy impact unless the answers to those questions are 1) Real/spectacular and 2) Yes, some. He's a top-five pick in FYPD depending on how you view pitching, though, and will probably be a top-40 prospect.

3
Liover Peguero   SS   OFP: 60   ETA: Late 2022/Early 2023
Born: 12/31/00   Age: 20   Bats: R   Throws: R   Height: 6'1"   Weight: 160
Origin: International Free Agent, 2017

The Report: Peguero stands out right away for the verve he brings onto the diamond. Then his batting practice starts, and he stands out for loud, hard contact. The swing is incredibly short, but he has elite hand/wrist strength that allows him to punish baseballs. Peguero is still prone to chase, but the barrel control is strong enough that he can get to most pitches thrown his way. He does not cut the most physical figure on the field, but as a player who just turned 20, he already has most of his man strength. Oh, he is also a plus runner with above-average arm strength in the field. Most of the mistakes I have seen from him at shortstop can be ironed out over time and with more defensive reps—not getting enough on a throw, being too casual, going too fast when not needed.

Development Track: Peguero may partner up with Gonzales as the everyday double play combination for Low-A Bradenton in 2021. He could also be pushed more aggressively since he is Rule 5 eligible after next season and is an obvious protection candidate. A full-season worth of games can have Peguero shoot up next year's Pirates list and into the Top 101.

Variance: Medium. There are enough tools here that even if he moves off SS, he will find an above-average defensive position somewhere. The home run power may be less than you would hope given his frame but this is still nearly a five-tool player, and tools play.

Mark Barry's Fantasy Take: Reason 2,304,283 that I'm mad about 2020 is that it deprived us of seeing Peguero's progression in Pittsburgh. The dude makes a ton of contact and could even see some of those high-contact batted balls wind up over the fence. He reminds me a little of Jean Segura or Whit Merrifield (minus some steals), and while those aren't overly sexy names, they still keep Peguero in the top-75 dynasty prospects or so.

4
Quinn Priester   RHP   OFP: 60   ETA: 2023
Born: 09/15/00   Age: 20   Bats: R   Throws: R   Height: 6'3"   Weight: 195
Origin: Round 1, 2019 Draft (#18 overall)

The Report: As one evaluator during instructs put it, "He looks like a young Gerritt Cole with blonde hair". This is rather high praise, but fits in some regards. Priester has obvious physical similarities, looking much more imposing than his listed 6-foot-3, 195 lbs. The fastball velocity has climbed as a pro, now comfortably sitting 95 and touching as high as 97. He throws strikes with the heater and repeats his delivery well, The breaking ball isn't a slider, instead a firm 12-6 curve in the low-80s with quality depth. He located the breaker with ease in my viewing. Plus grades on the fastball and curve are well within reach and could end up as high as plus-plus for both. The gains Priester has made since his name was first written in these pages last year have come ahead of schedule.

Development Track: Not that he would've likely thrown 130+ innings in Low-A ball in 2020, but yeah, full-season innings would've been nice. The physical gains that Priester has made has translated to stuff on the mound, leading to an overall diminished projection. The velocity gains need to be put to the test over a long season and full workload, as does the strike-throwing.

Variance: High. Priester is a recent first-round selection with obviously projectable stuff he has already started to realize. There will be a future for him, as well as quite a long development leash as a starting pitcher.

Mark Barry's Fantasy Take: I wrote last season that Priester was pretty far away and amounted to a dart throw for dynasty managers. While he's reportedly made some improvements since, not a lot has changed with his timeline. Still, I'd add him in super-deep leagues, or keep him on the watchlist for anything shallower.

5 **Brennan Malone** **RHP**   OFP: 60   ETA: 2024
Born: 09/08/00   Age: 20   Bats: R   Throws: R   Height: 6'4"   Weight: 205
Origin: Round 1, 2019 Draft (#33 overall)

The Report/Developmental Track: One of the most physically mature prep pitchers you'll ever see, Malone was settling nicely into the D'backs' organization after being selected 33rd overall, even getting into a playoff race game with short-season Hillsboro. He was then part of the package shipped to the Pirates in the Starling Marte deal, and by all accounts was set to take off in 2020. The filled-out 6-foot-5 frame delivers plenty of velocity into the mid-90s and three distinct secondary pitches that could each be weapons in the future. Everything about his profile screams workhorse starter.

Variance: Very High. You hate to see young pitchers miss out on the first full season of development. (insert guy shrugging emoji)

Mark Barry's Fantasy Take: There's a chance that Malone could eventually outpace Priester, but ultimately I have more faith in Priester's secondaries. Malone still has big strikeout upside, I'm just not interested beyond leagues with 200+ prospects.

6 **Tahnaj Thomas** **RHP**   OFP: 55   ETA: 2023/2024
Born: 06/16/99   Age: 22   Bats: R   Throws: R   Height: 6'4"   Weight: 190
Origin: International Free Agent, 2016

The Report: After being traded to the Pirates from Cleveland during the 2018 offseason, Thomas quickly found success the following year in the Appalachian League, posting career-best numbers across the board. The former infielder hurled 48 1/3 innings across 12 starts and pitched to a 3.17 ERA with 59 strikeouts against 14 walks. The stuff matched the stats in this case. Thomas' fastball sits in the mid-to-high-90s and can touch triple digits with plus ride. In 2020, he became more comfortable throwing the pitch at the top of the zone and focused on command to all four quadrants. The slider also took a step forward as he gained better feel for the offering and began using it in a wider variety of counts. Once Thomas deploys those two pitches with more consistent efficiency, the changeup will need to be addressed. The development of the change will determine the ultimate role for him, but the stuff projects to have late-inning impact if he does end up in the bullpen.

Development Track: Thomas has only been a full-time pitcher since 2017, so he is still a ways away from mapping out a definitive time table—his 48 1/3 innings in 2019 were a career high after all. Depending on where the Pirates assign Thomas at the beginning of the 2021 season—seemingly either the complex league or Low-A Bradenton—will be a good clue to where he is developmentally.

Variance: Extreme. Although Thomas has made solid progress over the last two years, players who go from the field to the mound have tons of risk. Plus, there is still a nice chunk of development left. Check back in a year, or two.

Mark Barry's Fantasy Take: My pal J.P. Breen loves Thomas. I like Thomas fine, but wish we had more to go on. Pitchers are notoriously risky, but I'd much rather take a shot on a guy like Thomas, who definitely has impact upside.

7 **Travis Swaggerty   OF**   OFP: 55   ETA: Late 2021 / Early 2022
Born: 08/19/97   Age: 23   Bats: L   Throws: L   Height: 5'11"   Weight: 180
Origin: Round 1, 2018 Draft (#10 overall)

The Report: At times in 2019 Swaggerty struggled, but he finished the second half on a strong note, as he slashed .306/.375/.430 over his final 63 games in the rough offensive environment of Bradenton. He made adjustments controlling his forward movement, getting to his hitting position on time more and honing in his launch position. With these positive progressions, paired with his approach and bat control, a continued, if delayed, surge could happen in 2021. In the outfield, Swaggerty's instincts and speed make him a plus center fielder. Additionally, in 2019 he swiped 23 bags in the Florida State League, tied for fifth in the circuit, which, along with his defense, will be his two most notable calling cards in the majors.

Development Track: So far, the Pirates have been fairly aggressive with the former first rounder. After scuffling at the end of 2018 in the South Atlantic League, Swaggerty was sent to High-A Bradenton to begin 2019. So an assignment to start 2021 in Double-A Altoona, or even Triple-A Indianapolis after competing at the alternate site, to test Swaggerty's revamped swing wouldn't be a shock, especially given the way he finished 2019.

Variance: Medium. The glove and speed tools should carry Swaggerty to an outfield bench role in the bigs. How much impact he has with the bat is the question here.

Mark Barry's Fantasy Take: It will be very interesting to see how Swaggerty's adjustments will carry over to competitive action. He already has a solid fantasy skillset with contact/speed, and if he can add anything to it, that's a super playable profile. I'd be making some inquiries on Swaggerty before we kick off the 2021 campaign, because if he starts out the season hitting, he won't be cheap.

8   **Cal Mitchell**   RF   OFP: 55   ETA: 2022
Born: 03/08/99   Age: 22   Bats: L   Throws: L   Height: 6'0"   Weight: 209
Origin: Round 2, 2017 Draft (#50 overall)

The Report: If we were doing our old The Good/The Bad format, we'd list "The Good" here as the hit and power tools and "The Bad" as basically everything else. Mitchell has an effortless and compact swing from the left side, enough to project to a plus hit tool if the plate approach holds up. He has plus power and the ball jumps off his bat. Of course, the "if" is carrying a lot of weight there; he ran a 142/32 K/BB ratio in High-A in 2019, and he was much too aggressive against offspeed pitches there. Mitchell's not going to produce much defensive value, so the bat is going to have to carry him, and while we still like the swing a lot, he's coming off a mediocre year and then a nearly lost one.

Development Track: We don't have much new to say on Mitchell. He was bypassed for the alternate site, which is telling us a little something; he was at instructs in the fall, but we didn't get any particularly notable feedback on his performance there. He should get a crack at Double-A in 2021.

Variance: High. We didn't get a better handle on the hit tool risk in 2020.

Mark Barry's Fantasy Take: I'm super into Good Hit and Power Tools for fantasy, because defense, shmeefense. However, I am extremely not into striking out nearly 30 percent of the time at High-A. I wouldn't write anyone off at 21 years old, but Mitchell is off my radar for now.

9   **Cody Bolton**   RHP   OFP: 55   ETA: Late 2021/Early 2022
Born: 06/19/98   Age: 23   Bats: R   Throws: R   Height: 6'3"   Weight: 185
Origin: Round 6, 2017 Draft (#178 overall)

The Report: Bolton began 2019 with High-A Bradenton and absolutely shoved, where he compiled a 1.61 ERA with 69 strikeouts over 61 2/3 innings, which led to a midseason promotion to Double-A Altoona. While there, however, Bolton struggled mightily in his nine starts, getting victimized by the long ball. To bounce back from the rough stretch, Bolton needs to improve pitch execution for all three offerings, especially working on his changeup development, as that pitch lagged behind the fastball and slider in 2019. Bolton's fastball sits in the low-to-mid-90s showing some cut and life to it, while the slider is a power breaker in the high-80s with average command that he pairs with the fastball well. He made some strides with his changeup at the alternate site, but needs to continue to work on starting it in the zone and getting it to consistently turn over to make it the needed third pitch in the arsenal.

Development Track: Given Bolton's struggles in his first Altoona stint there's a chance he returns to the Eastern League in 2021. He will only turn 23 next season, so there isn't a need to rush him to the bullpen yet, but to stay a starter long term, he will need to keep developing the changeup and add more innings to his ledger.

Variance: Medium. As mentioned above, the fastball and slider will play at the highest level and should earn Bolton a late-inning role in the bigs. Although, a mid-rotation starter projection is still in play for now.

Mark Barry's Fantasy Take: I think Bolton is probably a reliever, so he doesn't need to be on your radar until he lands a ninth-inning job.

10 **Max Kranick RHP**   OFP: 50   ETA: Late 2022/Early 2023
Born: 07/21/97   Age: 23   Bats: R   Throws: R   Height: 6'3"   Weight: 175
Origin: Round 11, 2016 Draft (#345 overall)

The Report: Although Kranick has battled injury problems the last couple of years, the righty has pitched well and thrown strikes when he's been on the mound. During the quarantine year, he made a mechanical change while keeping his velocity in the mid-90s. Besides injury concerns, inducing whiffs has been another knock on Kranick. This past year, however, he began missing bats at a higher rate, as his secondaries showed more effectiveness than they had before. The changeup, sitting in the mid-80s, is deceptive out of the hand, and he shows a slider look in the low-80s and a cutter look in the upper-80s. It's not a flashy profile but Kranick does enough things well.

Development Track: Even with the injury problems, Kranick has steadily increased his innings over the years, peaking at 109 1/3 in 2019 with High-A Bradenton. From all indications, he held his own at the alternate site in Altoona this year against advanced hitters. So Kranick should be set to return there in 2021 as a Double-A starter. If the ability to miss bats continues in games next year, Kranick could push for a quick promotion. Although he will need to stay healthy long enough.

Variance: High. He throws strikes at a high rate but the injury bug is still worrisome. Until he can show signs of better durability the variance will stay. However, the report from this year is intriguing.

Mark Barry's Fantasy Take: Intriguing, yes. Kranick should be widely available if/when he gets called up, so you can make a decision then. I'm not sure he's more than a streamer.

The Prospects You Meet Outside The Top Ten

MLB arms, but less upside than you'd like

Carmen Mlodzinski   RHP   Born: 02/19/99   Age: 22   Bats: R   Throws: R   Height: 6'2"   Weight: 232   Origin: Round 1, 2020 Draft (#31 overall)

Scouts had been witnessing the pure stuff for years, yet the performances and injuries kept the true potential from doing more than flashing. Finally healthy, Mlodzinski had a very strong performance at the Cape and backed that up again with another solid spring before the shutdown. His fastball is a power sinker with good movement that gets up to 95 and is located much better to his glove-side—which hitters began picking up on. He'll need to get more comfortable moving his spots around and working on his changeup to play off the sinker movement. If not, there is some reliever risk with his slider/cutter being just average as his preferred offspeed pitch.

Blake Cederlind   RHP   Born: 01/04/96   Age: 25   Bats: R   Throws: R   Height: 6'4"   Weight: 205   Origin: Round 5, 2016 Draft (#165 overall)

If it seems like we've been writing a lot of 95-and-a-slider relievers this year, well, Cederlind's a 100-and-a-cutter guy, so that's at least a little different. He sits high-90s and touches triple-digits with a two-seam fastball that has some nasty sink on it. His "offspeed" pitch is a cutter that gets up into the low-90s. He put it together very quickly in 2019 and kept it going at the end of the 2020 season at the majors; he's got a chance to get into high-leverage work very quickly

Wil Crowe   RHP   Born: 09/09/94   Age: 26   Bats: R   Throws: R   Height: 6'2"   Weight: 228   Origin: Round 2, 2017 Draft (#65 overall)

Dealt to the Pirates as part of the Josh Bell trade, Crowe is a major-league-ready utility arm, who has never really shown enough stuff or durability to project as an average starter. His low-90s fastball is a little too hittable due to fringy command and only occasional sink. He leaned heavily on his slider in his 2020 MLB cameo, and it might end up a tick above average. There's a curve and change as well. Crowe was unlikely to get much major-league run in Washington, but he could fulfill a variety of roles for the Pirates.

Prospects to dream on a little

Jared Jones   RHP   Born: 08/06/01   Age: 19   Bats: L   Throws: R   Height: 6'1"   Weight: 180   Origin: Round 2, 2020 Draft (#44 overall)

One of the most electric arms in the draft regardless of age, Jones has one of the largest ranges of possible career outcomes. Working a heater in the upper-90s—with a lot of effort, mind you—and a snapping power curveball, it looks like the kind of stuff you see at the back-end of a bullpen right now in the majors, none in a recently drafted 19-year-old. Despite all that effort, he actually shows quite good body control, varying his delivery motion to mess with hitters trying to cheat early on the velocity. The two questions he'll face developmentally are whether he can throw enough strikes and if a third pitch can be brought along.

Mason Martin   1B   Born: 06/02/99   Age: 22   Bats: L   Throws: R   Height: 6'0"   Weight: 201   Origin: Round 17, 2017 Draft (#508 overall)
Sporting prodigious power from the left side, Martin smacked 35 homers across both A-ball levels in 2019, but struck out 168 times in 556 plate appearances. He also drew 68 walks so this feels like a boom-or-bust, three true outcomes profile. Reducing those strikeout numbers, by having him hone in and be more aggressive in his hitting zone, will be crucial going forward.

Matthew Fraizer   OF   Born: 01/12/98   Age: 23   Bats: L   Throws: R   Height: 6'3"   Weight: 205   Origin: Round 3, 2019 Draft (#95 overall)
After suffering a hamate injury prior the 2019 draft, Fraizer struggled in the New York Penn League, slashing .221/.287/.266 in 43 games. One issue was his contact point, which led into another, his launch angle. The return on the work in instructs has so far improved the chances of Fraizer finding some power in the stroke. How much of that will be gap-to-gap and how much over-the-fence power will need to be demonstrated in 2021.

Eddy Yean   RHP   Born: 06/25/01   Age: 20   Bats: R   Throws: R   Height: 6'1"   Weight: 180   Origin: International Free Agent, 2017
The other half of the Josh Bell trade return, Yean is an undersized righty with some feel for a changeup. His velocity ticked up in 2020, but he hasn't pitched above the complex level, and we haven't seen the velocity stick in a real season yet. Check back in this space in a year.

José Soriano   RHP   Born: 10/20/98   Age: 22   Bats: R   Throws: R   Height: 6'3"   Weight: 220   Origin: International Free Agent, 2016
The Pirates used the first overall pick in the 2020 Rule 5 draft to pluck arguably the best overall prospect left unprotected. Soriano hasn't pitched above A-ball and will spend at least the first few months of 2021 recovering and rehabbing from Tommy John surgery, but if healthy he could soak up some 'pen innings for the Pirates, and they might come out the other side with a potential average MLB starter or setup guy down the line given the potentially above-average fastball/curve combo.

Rodolfo Castro   2B   Born: 05/21/99   Age: 22   Bats: S   Throws: R   Height: 6'0"   Weight: 200   Origin: International Free Agent, 2015
Castro has some interesting pieces in his game; pro scouts have pegged him as a favorite to us going back to 2018. He's a switch-hitter who takes loose swings that are well-suited for power both in the gaps and over the fences. Primarily a second

baseman, he can play all around the dirt. The downside is his pitch recognition, and that limits the hit tool presently. Castro was at the alternate site and added to the 40-man this offseason even though he's never played above A-ball, and the team liked his development this season.

Top Talents 25 and Under (as of 4/1/2021):

1. Ke'Bryan Hayes, 3B
2. Nick Gonzales, IF
3. Mitch Keller, RHP
4. Liover Peguero, SS
5. Quinn Priester, RHP
6. Brennan Malone, RHP
7. Bryan Reynolds, OF
8. Tahnaj Thomas, RHP
9. Travis Swaggerty, OF
10. Cole Tucker, SS

Mitch Keller's 2020 performance was the opposite of his 2019: shiny ERA (2.91), awful underlying rates (7.06 DRA and more walks than strikeouts). It feels like we've been writing about Keller's inconsistency and wavering command since the earth started spinning, but somehow he only has 69 2/3 MLB innings; he missed a bunch of time in 2020 with oblique problems. He continued down the 2019 path as a fastball/slider/curve pitcher when he was on the mound, only throwing his changeup 3.4 percent of the time. My cheeky past prediction that he'll be a future Rays ace after a change of scenery trade and better pitch design is a year closer to reality, if nothing else.

If you had told me that Bryan Reynolds would hit .280/.349/.463 over his first two seasons in the majors, I'd have thought he'd be higher than this. But after a fourth place in the 2019 Rookie of the Year race, Reynolds fell flat on his face in 2020, hitting .189 with an 87 DRC+. That's not going to cut it in a corner, though the Pirates will certainly run it back and hope that 2020 is the small sample fluke instead of 2019.

Cole Tucker needs to hit a little more to fill his destiny as a second-division shortstop. Luckily, he's on a second-division franchise.

Part 3: Featured Articles

Pirates All-Time Top 10 Players

by Matthew Trueblood

POSITION PLAYERS

HONUS WAGNER, SS (1900-1917)

There was no phase of the game in which Wagner didn't dominate. He won games with his bat, with his glove, and with his legs. He revolutionized shortstop. Our modern minds struggle to contextualize his power, which was massive, because the dead ball ensured that his extra-base hits were mostly doubles and triples. More than some other stars of his era, he would accept an occasional strikeout for the chance to hit for power, and it was a worthy tradeoff for him. A question: why did no one ever think to call a much later Pirates great The Flying Dutchman?

ARKY VAUGHAN, SS (1932-1941)

The 1935 NL MVP voting is one of the great travesties in the history of the award. It's not that Gabby Hartnett was undeserving, and we might put a higher value on his performance now than we can with only rear-facing tools for catcher defense, but Vaughan had one of the great shortstop seasons in history (.385/.491/.607) and finished third. For the most part, Vaughan played shortstop because he could acquit himself there, but was not a standout defensively—he couldn't throw on the run but had to plant himself first. At the plate, though, he was a terror. He was exceptionally patient, leading the NL in walks three years in a row, and matched Waner for strikeout avoidance, all with plenty of pop. The combination of questions about his glove and a personality conflict with manager Frankie Frisch hastened his December 1941 trade to the Dodgers.

FRED CLARKE, OF (1900-1911, 1913-1915)

Already an established star for a moribund Louisville team that was folded into the Pittsburgh club, Clarke became a cornerstone for the Pirates after the quasi-merger that also landed Wagner and others in Pittsburgh. He was a balanced slugger, patient and powerful at the plate, yet able to shorten up and find the hole for hits when needed. He had a .926 OPS in the 1910 World Series, including two home runs, which lifted the Pirates to the title.

MAX CAREY, OF (1910-1926)

A patient, well-rounded switch-hitter and a fine defensive center fielder, the former seminary student delivered steady value for the Pirates for 15 years with his exceptional baserunning. He was a .267 career hitter through age 26 but hit .295 thereafter, a transformation that he began even before the introduction of the livelier baseball—he had swapped some of his hard contact for fewer strikeouts, a smart concession to age that fits nicely into his overall profile. Remembered as one of the National League's great leadoff men, the Pirates actually had him hitting second behind lesser talents Carson Bigbee and Rabbit Maranville for years. He led the NL in stolen bases 10 times and retired as the league's all-time leader in that category.

PAUL WANER, OF (1926-1940)

Waner kept the Dead Ball Era's flame alive, even though he didn't debut until it was dead and gone. He had above-average power, technically, but almost all of it came in the form of doubles and triples. His theory of hitting was that a batter should shoot for the foul lines—if it worked you'd have a double and if it didn't the ball would go foul and you'd get another chance. This idea only works if you have exceptional bat-control, which Waner did—he struck out less than half as often as the typical hitter of his day. He was a drinking man with a sense of humor about that and his declining eyesight—he once told a teammate he generally saw two balls at the plate and just swung at the bigger one—and somehow made it all work for him. He ran batting averages that stood out even in the batting average-crazy 1930s. From 1927-1937, he averaged 208 hits a year, and batted .349.

RALPH KINER, OF (1946-1953)

Kiner reached the Hall of Fame after appearing in only the minimum 10 seasons, his career delayed on the front end by military service in World War II (unlike many ballplayers, he didn't join a service team but was a flier in the Pacific theater) and back problems on the other. Winning home run titles in one's first seven seasons opens many doors. Kiner didn't hit for sensational averages, but in the immediate postwar period, he was a walks-and-homers machine unlike anything either league had seen since Babe Ruth's retirement. At the time, it was common practice to pick at Kiner's faults—his defense, baserunning, the way he hit home runs over a fence that had been pulled in for Hank Greenberg, his personality—and Branch Rickey famously slagged him to Pirates ownership so he could trade him and touch off a rebuild. The argument wasn't necessarily that 40-50 home runs a season didn't have value, but how much value did they have when one accounted for all the associated negatives, real or perceived? The conversation was unfair to Kiner, but in general terms it was worth having.

ROBERTO CLEMENTE, OF (1955-1972)

Clemente faced, in general, a softer, slipperier form of racism than Jackie Robinson, Larry Doby, and the other Black players who made up the first wave that re-integrated the major leagues. That only meant it was often harder for him to win support and convince the public that he was being mistreated; the harm still happened. Despite that, Clemente changed baseball in a deep, lasting, profoundly positive way. He played the game with an intensity that verged on rage and without shame in either emotion. He left ballparks buzzing with people trying to process his unique greatness. Our statistics, which leave Clemente off the plinth where Willie Mays, Hank Aaron, and Frank Robinson reside, are only telling on themselves.

WILLIE STARGELL, OF/1B (1962-1982)

Over 21 seasons, all with the Pirates, Stargell never played in 150 regular-season games in a single year. His knees were a perpetual problem and until he became a star his managers frequently benched him against left-handed starting pitchers. That Stargell made it through his tumultuous early career and became a beloved, All-Star slugger in his 30s is a testament to his determination. He encountered racism throughout his life, from a peripatetic childhood in which he also suffered abuse, abandonment, and malnourishment through a series of minor-league stops, and again in the majors. He often said he kept going out of fear of what awaited him if baseball didn't work out. He adjusted and benefited from the Pirates' move to Three Rivers Stadium, helping him amass the numbers that earned him induction to the Hall of Fame. As with Clemente, the numbers don't wholly capture his impact.

BARRY BONDS, OF (1986-1992)

He was a weak-armed left fielder, and he should have listened to Andy Van Slyke, who told him to move in before Francisco Cabrera struck the winning blow in the 1992 NLCS. He was not a good teammate, though sometimes his teammates were bad to him first. In every other sense, though, Bonds's time in Pittsburgh was a thrilling and fun ride. He had incredible speed and power and played with swagger. He forced opponents to throw strikes but hit them so hard that they often refused to do so. He should have won MVP awards in each of his final three years in Pittsburgh. What came after, with San Francisco, will always be problematic, but he was a Cooperstown-level talent in Pittsburgh too.

ANDREW McCUTCHEN, OF (2009-2017)

A great many body types can work in baseball, and different positions demand different ones, but McCutchen's is the perfect physique for the game: short, powerful, and with quick, evenly-proportioned limbs. At his best, he could accelerate quickly to make plays on the bases and in center field; turn on anyone's best heat, with a kinetic swing that seemed to lift him off the ground with its speed and spin; and wait long enough to tell balls from strikes before triggering that swing. His five truly great seasons (2011-15, total WARP: 24.6) gave the Pirates their brief respite from 30 years of drudgery. Despite a 2012 Gold Glove he was miscast in center field, but a common feature of bad teams is asking players to do more than they're capable of doing.

PITCHERS

SAM LEEVER, RHP (1898-1910)

The Goshen Schoolmaster's first full season was 1899, when he was 27. That was hardly uncommon, at the time, but it made for a short career. He pitched as often as they would let him, especially as a rookie, when he made 39 starts and finished 11 games as a reliever. Perhaps because of that heavy usage, his innings totals sagged over the ensuing three seasons, but he won the ERA title as the co-ace of the 1903 Pirates, who reached the first (true) World Series.

DEACON PHILLIPPE, RHP (1900-1911)

Joining Adams and Leever as the pitching stars for the early Pirates teams who went to the 1903 World Series and contended throughout the decade, Phillippe had the best control of any starter of that era. He had the lowest walk rate in the National League in five of six seasons from 1902-1907, passing just 1.2 batters per nine innings. When owner Barney Dreyfuss nimbly jumped from the sinking ship of his own Louisville team and bought the Pirates, Phillippe was one of the fistful of stars he brought with him to Pittsburgh. He won 20 or more games in five of six seasons from 1900 through 1905 with an overall ERA of 2.44, which was well below average. He started five of eight games in the 1903 World Series. In contrast, Cy Young himself started only three.

BABE ADAMS, RHP (1907, 1909-1916, 1918-1926)

The nickname "Babe" alluded to Adams's good looks, and he was quite a talker, too. In fact, he talked himself right off the team with an errant comment that was dimly supportive of a mild player rebellion in 1926. He'd be immensely popular in today's game, including with the sabermetric set, because he believed a lot of things about pitching with unusual conviction, and was never afraid to expound on them (he became a journalist after retirement, too). He claimed to throw 10 different kinds of curveball—Yu Darvish, eat your heart out. He had excellent control, too, walking just 1.3 batters per nine innings over the course of his career, peaking in 1920 when he passed just 18 batters in 263 innings. He rode that to a 2.48 ERA for the long span of 1909-22. But for a very strange late-career interregnum during which he lost effectiveness and the Pirates let him go back to the minors he might have stacked up career numbers as good as the other legends of that era.

WILBUR COOPER, LHP (1912-1924)

Cooper drew widespread praise for the apparent ease of his delivery and good control. His clean mechanics also made for clean bills of health, and Cooper averaged 300 innings pitched for seven seasons from 1917-1923. As easy-throwing hurlers today do, Cooper also got a reputation for having a sneaky fastball—one he might have helped along by using chewing tobacco to darken the baseball. He won 20 or more games in four out of five seasons from 1920 through 1924 with an aggregate ERA of 3.12. The year he failed to win 20 he led the NL in losses with 19, albeit with an ERA a half-run below league average.

RAY KREMER, RHP (1924-1933)

For a few years, Kremer was one of the best pitchers in baseball. He paced the National League in ERA in both 1926 and 1927. He didn't rack up strikeouts, but he dominated anyway. That might have lasted longer, had he not done virtually everything a pitcher can do to shorten their career. He worked as a reliever between starts, switched between an overhand delivery and a low-sidearm one within at-bats, used a screwball, and threw hard. About half a decade into his career, he was left primarily with a fading fastball, a good changeup, and a shorter, sharper version of his curve, and became a quantity-over-quality guy. Case in point: In 1930 he led the NL with 20 wins and 276 innings pitched, but he gave up 366 hits and his ERA was 5.02. It was a rabbit-ball year so the ERA wasn't as bad as it looks, but he wasn't good either.

RIP SEWELL, RHP (1938-1949)

Sewell is one of only a small handful of reliably good pitchers after the Deadball Era whose walks substantially outpaced their whiffs. How? His repertoire was absolutely insane, that's how. He had a sinker that was probably a splitter, a slider before anyone threw many sliders, and an overhand fastball. He also had an eephus (often referred to, in his case, as a "blooper") that allegedly reached 20 feet in the air on its rainbow arc to the plate. Unlike most guys who had such a pitch in their back pocket, he threw it quite often. The only time he had cause to regret it was in the 1946 All-Star Game when Ted Williams cheated up in the box and knocked it out of the park.

VERN LAW, RHP (1950-1967)

A well-rounded athlete, Law was used as a pinch-hitter a dozen times in his career and as a pinch-runner twice that often. He hit .216/.254/.309 with 11 home runs for his career, quite good for a pitcher in an offense-starved era. On the rubber he showcased two distinct breaking balls that he could consistently throw for strikes. Control pitchers are a Pirates tradition and Law was part of that lineage with an average of just 1.7 unintentional walks per nine over the course of his career. His attacking style led to home-run trouble, but he stayed out of it for a couple years and won a Cy Young Award for the champion Pirates in 1960. The Pirates picked his bespectacled son Vance in the 39th round in 1978, suggesting the selection was more for sentimentality's sake than belief in his potential, but he played well in the minors, made his major league debut with the team in 1980, and went on to have a decent career as a third baseman and utilityman.

BOB FRIEND, RHP (1951-1965)

Using a Tiant-esque twist that took his gaze out toward left field just before delivering the ball, Friend made for an incredibly uncomfortable at-bat. He had a power sinker which became famous for breaking bats as it rode in on right-handed hitters, and he held them to a career line of .258/.295/.372. His breaking ball was a subject of constant fascination: It was a hard curve when he came up, but he could change its shape and speed. Over time, he claimed to add a slider—only he claimed to do so several times. It might be that he just tinkered with grips and slid up and down the breaking-ball spectrum throughout his career.

BOB VEALE, LHP (1962-1972)

Big, hard-throwing, and wild as hell, Veale had to be a scary matchup for hitters. Hitters generated very little power against him (he gave up 0.4 home runs per nine innings in his career), not only because of the power in his fastball and slider but because of the wildness that put them on the defensive. Through 1970, when his stuff went over the inevitable cliff, Veale had a 2.95 ERA. From his debut in 1962 through that season, only Bob Gibson, Sam McDowell, Juan Marichal, and Jim Bunning struck out more batters.

JOHN CANDELARIA, LHP (1975-1985, 1993)

The year that put Candelaria on the map was 1977, his second full campaign. He won 20 games, pitched 231 innings, and took home the ERA title. Here's the weird thing: he also gave up more home runs than any other pitcher in the National League. That's an odd pair of leaderboards to top, but Candelaria (the six-foot-seven lefty with the funky facial hair) was an odd, eye-catching pitcher. Thereafter, the Candy Man evolved into a control artist, and settled in as a solid swingman and occasional mid-rotation starter.

A Taxonomy of 2020 Abnormalities

by Rob Mains

I'm going to start this with a trivia question. Trust me, it's relevant. Don't bother skipping to the end of the article to find the answer, it's not there.

Only five players have appeared in 140 or more games for 16 straight seasons. Who are they?

It's a trivia question starting off an essay, so you know how this works: Whatever you guessed, you're wrong. It's okay. As someone who purchased this book, chances are good that you're an educated baseball fan. But the circumstances behind 2020 force us to abandon, or at least seriously question, some of our favorite patterns and crutches for evaluating the game we love.

We just completed what was undoubtedly the strangest season in MLB history. No fans, geographically limited schedule, universal DH, seven-inning twin bills, runners on second in extra innings, a 16-team postseason, a club playing at a Triple-A stadium. Some of these changes will likely persist (sorry), but we've never had so many tweaks dumped on us all at once, at least not since they figured out how many balls were in a walk.

And the biggest, of course, was the 60-game season. The 19th century was dotted with teams that went bankrupt before the season ended, but the lone season with only 60 scheduled games was 1877. That year there were only six teams, the league rostered a total of 77 players (just 16 more than the 2020 Marlins), and batters called for pitches to be thrown high or low by the pitcher, who was 50 feet away. We can say the 2020 season was easily the shortest ever for recognizable baseball.

As such, it'll stand out. Few abbreviated seasons do. Just about everybody reading this knows the 1994 season ended after Seattle's Randy Johnson struck out Oakland's Ernie Young for the last out of the Mariners-A's game on August 11. The ensuing player strike wiped out the rest of the season and the postseason. Teams played only 112-117 games that year.

And many of you know that a strike in the middle of the 1981 season split the season in two, resulting in the only Division Series until 1995. Teams played only 103-111 games that year, the shortest regular season since 1885.

Those two seasons are memorable. So when we see that nobody drove in 100 runs in 1981, or that Greg Maddux was the only pitcher with 180 or more innings pitched in 1994, we think, "Of course. Strike year."

But we don't remember other short years. You might not recall that the 1994 strike spilled into the next year, chopping 18 games off the 1995 schedule. You might've read that the 1918 season, played during the last pandemic, ended after Labor Day due to the government's World War I "work or fight" order. A strike erased the first week and a half of the 1972 season, but that year's best known as the last time pitchers batted in the American League.

The point is, while we don't remember small changes to the schedule, we remember the big ones. The 1981 mid-season strike. The 1994 season- and Series-ending strike. And, of course, the pandemic-shortened 2020 season. We won't need a reminder why Marcell Ozuna's 18 homers were the fewest to lead the National League in a century. (Literally; Cy Williams led with 15 in 1920.)

Now, about that trivia question. The five players are Hank Aaron, Brooks Robinson, Pete Rose, Ichiro Suzuki, and Johnny Damon. The one nobody gets, of course, is Damon, and a lot of people miss Ichiro, whose last season of 140-plus games came garbed in the red-orange and ocean blue of Miami when he was 42. That's half of what makes it a good question. The other half is the two guys whom many think made the list but didn't. Lou Gehrig? His streak started in the Yankees' 42nd game of the 1925 season and lasted only 13 seasons after that. And everybody assumes Cal Ripken Jr. did it, having played 2,632 straight games over 17 seasons. But one of those 17 seasons was 1994, when the Orioles played only 112 games.

My point? *I just told you* everybody remembers the 1994 strike year, but everybody forgets it fell in the middle of Ripken's streak, separating the first twelve years from the last four. Just because we recall something doesn't mean it's always at the front of our minds.

Nobody is going to forget 2020, and baseball is obviously not the main reason. But there will come a time in the future when you're looking at a player's or a team's record, and there will be baffling numbers there for 2020, and you'll think, "I wonder what happened." (Not to mention the missing line for minor league players.) Just like you forgot that the 1994 strike limited Ripken to 112 games.

Try not to forget it, though. The 2020 season resulted in weird statistical results for several reasons.

There were only 60 games.
I know, duh. But that had impacts beyond counting stats like Ozuna's home run total or Yu Darvish and Shane Bieber leading the majors with eight wins. (I know, pitcher wins, but still.)

The 162-game season is the longest among major North American sports, and that duration gives us a gift. Over the course of a long season, small variations tend to even out. A player who has a ten-game hot streak will probably have a ten-game cold streak. A team that starts the year losing a bunch of close games will probably win a bunch of them. We get regression to the mean. Statistics stabilize.

Consider flipping a coin. Over the long run, we expect it to come up heads about half the time. But the fewer flips, the more variation there'll be. If you flip a coin six times, probability theory tells us you'll get at least two-third heads about 34 percent of the time. Flip it 30 times, your chance of two-thirds heads drops to five percent.

Or, relevant to this case, if you flip a coin 60 times, your chance of getting at least 36 heads—that's 60 percent—is 7.75 percent. Expand the coin-flipping to 162 times, and the chance of getting 60 percent heads drops to 0.73 percent.

In other words, the odds of an outcome that's 20 percent better (or worse) than expected is *more than ten times higher* when you flip your coin 60 times than when you do it 162 times. Call it small sample size, call lack of mean reversion, or call it luck not evening out, 162 is a lot more predictive than 60. You get much more variation over 60 games than over 162. Bieber's 1.63 ERA and 0.87 FIP aren't something we'd see over a full season, and neither is Javier Baéz's .203/.238/.360.

Some players' lines in 2020 look normal. Brian Anderson had an .811 OPS in 2019 and an .810 OPS in 2020. (He probably would have gotten that last point if he'd been given enough time.) But there are many like Bieber and Baéz, some of them from young players still establishing their talent levels. The answer to the question, "What went right or wrong for that guy in 2020?" is most likely "Nothing, it was just a 2020 thing."

Preseason training was abbreviated for hitters.

Every year, spring training drags. Players get tired of it, fans get tired of it, and you sure can tell sportswriters get tired of it. Yes, something to get everyone into shape is necessary, but does it really have to drag on for over a month? Can't we shorten it?

The 2020 season answered in the negative, at least for hitters. Warren Spahn is credited with saying that hitting is timing and pitching is upsetting timing. It appears nobody had his timing down after the abbreviated July summer camp. Through August 9—18 games into the season—MLB batters were hitting .230/.311/.395 with a .275 BABIP. That BABIP, had it held, would have been the lowest since 1968, the Year of the Pitcher. In recent years it's hovered around .300.

It didn't hold. Play returned to more normal levels the rest of the year: .249/.325/.425 with a .297 BABIP starting August 10. But batters whose play concentrated in those first two weeks wound up with ugly lines. Andrew

Benintendi went on the injured list with a season-ending rib cage strain on August 11. His final line: .103/.314/.128 in 14 games. Franchy Cordero went on the IL with a hamate bone fracture on August 9 and a .154/.185/.231 line. Even though he came back strong in a late September return, it was too late to repair his full-season numbers.

Preseason training was abbreviated for pitchers.

Every year, spring training drags. Players get tired of it, fans get tired of it … wait, I already said that. But the abbreviated preseason was tough on pitchers, too. As noted, they had the upper hand coming out of the gate. But then they lost that hand. And then their arms, too.

The 2020 season was spread over 67 days. During those 67 days, 237 pitchers hit the Injured List, compared to 135 in the first 67 days of 2019. A lot of those IL stints, though, were COVID-19-related. Still, over the first 67 days of the 2019 season, there were 72 pitchers on the IL with arm injuries. That figure jumped to 110 in 2020, a 53 percent increase.

There are a number of factors contributing to pitcher arm injuries, ranging from usage to velocity, but it appears that attenuated preseason training played a role. A lot of pitchers had super-short seasons due to arm woes. Corey Kluber, Roberto Osuna, and Shohei Ohtani combined for seven innings, none after August 8. All suffered arm injuries. We'll never know whether they'd have fared better with a longer preseason, but we can guess how they probably feel.

Everybody played.

Rosters were set to expand from 25 to 26 in 2020, so even if we'd had a normal season, we'd have likely seen 2019's record of 1,410 players on MLB rosters broken. But due to the pandemic, rosters started the year at 30 and were cut to only 28. Add multiple COVID-19 absences and the revolving door caused by poor starts by hitters and a rash of pitcher arm injuries, and 1,289 players appeared in MLB games in 2020. The comparable figure over the first 67 days of the 2019 season was 1,109. That 16 percent increase works out to an average of six more players per team in 2020 compared to a similar slice of 2019. A future look back at 2020 rosters will include a lot of unfamiliar names.

Plus became a minus.

In advanced metrics, we adjust batter and pitcher performance for park and league/era variations. A plus sign appended to the end of a measure means that it's adjusted for park and league. It's scaled to an average of 100, with higher figures above average and lower figures below average. (Similarly, a metric with a minus is also park- and league-adjusted and scaled to 100, with lower values better.) Here at BP, our advanced measure of offensive performance is DRC+. Baseball-Reference has OPS+ and FanGraphs has wRC+.

Using park and league adjustments, we can compare Dante Bichette's 1995 Steroid Era season at pre-humidor Coors Field (.340/.364/.620, 40 homers, 128 RBI, MVP runner-up) with Jim Wynn's 1968 Year of the Pitcher season at the cavernous Astrodome (.269/.376/.474, 26 homers, 67 RBI, no MVP votes). It's not close. DRC+, OPS+, and wRC+ all give the nod to Wynn, handily. This is a useful tool. As my Baseball Prospectus colleague Patrick Dubuque tweeted last fall, "Please note that when I ask how you are, I am already adjusting for era."

The 2020 season messes up plus (and minus) stats for two reasons. First, the park adjustment was based on only 30 home games instead of the usual 81. Everything noted above regarding the short season applies, literally doubly, to park effect calculations. DRC+ uses a single-season park factor. OPS+ uses a three-year average and wRC+ five years. The figure for 2020 is suspect.

Second, OPS+ and wRC+ adjust for league: American and National. (DRC+ adjusts for opponent, regardless of league.) While there were two leagues in 2020, they were an artificial construct. To reduce travel, teams played opponents geographically, not based on league. There weren't two leagues, American and National. There were three, Western, Central, and Eastern.

That makes a difference because teams in the same league played in different run-scoring environments. AL teams scored 4.58 runs per game, NL teams 4.71. That's a small difference. But teams in the East scored 0.21 more runs per game (4.95) than teams in the West (4.74), and they both scored a lot more than Central teams (4.25). Adjusting for league misses that difference, so this book will be safe in that regard, but other sources may be distorted somewhat.

Not every game was a "game."

In 2020, the rising tide of strikeouts was finally stemmed. Strikeouts per team per game fell from 8.8 in 2019 to 8.7 in 2020. That marked the first decline after 14 straight annual increases.

In 2020, the rising tide of strikeouts rose higher. Batters struck out in 23.4 percent of plate appearances compared to 23.0 percent in 2019. That marked the 15th straight annual increase.

Both are true statements.

Because of two rule changes—seven-inning doubleheaders and runners on second in extra innings—games in 2020 were unprecedented in their brevity. There were 37.0 plate appearances per game in 2020. The only years with fewer were 1904 and 1906-1909. The average game in 2020 entailed 8.61 innings pitched, the fewest since 1899.

So when you see any per-game stats for 2020, you need to increase them by 3 or 4 percent to get them on equal footing with recent years.

Or, better, just ignore them. Last year happened. There were major league games contested between major league teams. But when you're looking at those physical or electronic baseball cards, when you're weaving narratives over why this young player's inevitable rise to stardom fell apart or why that old veteran rekindled his magic, don't linger on the 2020 line. It was just too weird.

Thanks to Lucas Apostoleris for research assistance.

—Rob Mains is an author of Baseball Prospectus.

Tranches of WAR

by Russell A. Carleton

We ask "replacement level" to be a lot of things. Sometimes contradictory things. Sometimes I wonder if we know what it even means anymore. The original idea was that it represented the level of production that a team could expect to get from "freely available talent", including bench players, minor leaguers, and waiver wire pickups. It created a common benchmark to compare everyone to, and for that reason, it represented an advancement well beyond what was available at the time. In fact, it created a language and a framework for evaluating players that was not just better but *entirely* different than what came before it.

But then we started mumbling in that language. The idea behind "wins above replacement" was one part sci-fi episode and one part mathematical exercise. Imagine that a player had disappeared before the season and suddenly, in an alternate timeline, his team would have had to replace him. The distance between him and that replacement line was his value. We need to talk about that alternate timeline.

Without getting too into 2:00 am "deep conversations" with extensive navel-gazing, it's worth thinking about why one player might not be playing, while another might.

- A player might not be playing because he has a short-term injury or his manager believes that he needs a day off.
- A player might not be playing because he has a longer-term injury that requires him to be on the injured list.

There's a difference here between these two situations. In particular, the first one generally *doesn't* involve a compensatory roster move, while the second one does. It's possible, though not guaranteed, that the person who will be replacing the injured/resting player would be the same in either case. That matters. Teams generally carry a spare part for all eight position players on the diamond, although in the era of a four-player bench, those spare parts usually are the backup plan for more than one spot.

A couple of years ago, I posed a hypothetical question. Suppose that a team had two players in its system fighting for a fourth outfielder spot. One of them was a league average hitter, but would be worth 20 runs below average if allowed to play center field for a full season. One of them was a perfectly average fielder, but would be 15 runs below average as a hitter, if allowed to play an entire season. Which of the two should the team roster? It's tempting to say the second one, as overall, he is the better player. That misses the point. A league average hitter on the bench isn't just a potential replacement for an injured outfielder. He might also pinch hit for the light-hitting shortstop in a key spot. You keep the average hitter on the roster, even though he isn't a hand-in-glove fit for one specific place on the field, because being a bench player is a different job description than being a long-term fill-in for someone. If you find yourself in need of a longer-term fill-in, you can bring the other guy up from AAA.

When we're determining the value of an everyday player though, if he had disappeared before the season and a team would have had to replace his production, they likely would have done it with a player who was a long-term fill-in type because they would have had to replace a guy who played everyday. Maybe that's the same guy that they would have rostered on their bench anyway, but we don't know. It gets to the query of what we hope to accomplish with WAR. Are we looking for an accurate modeling of reality or are we looking for a common baseline to compare everyone to? Both have their uses, but they are somewhat different questions.

Let's talk about another dichotomy.

- A player might not be playing because he isn't very good and is a bench-level player.
- A player might not be playing because there is another player on the team who has a situational advantage that makes him the better choice today. The classic case of this is a handedness platoon. On another day, he might be a better choice.

When we think about player usage, I think we're still stuck in the model that there are starters and there are scrubs. We have plenty of words for bench players or reserves or backups or utility guys. We do still have the word "platoon" in our collective vocabulary, but in the age of short benches, it's hard to construct one. It's always been hard to construct them. You have to find two players who hit with different hands, have skill sets that complement each other, and probably play the same position. In the era of the short bench, one of them had probably better double as a utility player in some way. Baseball has a two-tiered language geared toward the idea of regulars and reserves. The fact that it was so easy for me to find plenty of synonyms for "a player whose primary function is to come into a game to replace a regular player if he is injured or resting" should tell you something.

I'm always one to look for "unspoken words" in baseball. What is it called when someone is both half of a platoon and the utility infielder? That guy exists sometimes, but he reveals himself in that role—usually by accident. We don't have a word for that, and whenever I find myself saying "we don't have a word for that", I look for new opportunities. What do you call it, further, when the job of being the utility infielder is decentralized across the whole infield with occasional contributions from the left fielder? It's not even a "super-utility" player. What happens when you build your entire roster around the idea that everyone will be expected to be a triple major?

⚾   ⚾   ⚾

I think someone else beat me to this one, and on a grand scale. Platoons work because we know that hitters of the opposite hand to the pitcher get better results than hitters of the same hand, usually to the tune of about 20 points of OBP. If you want to express that in runs, it usually comes out to somewhere around 10 to 12 runs of linear weights value prorated across 650 PA. But hang on a second, now let's say that we have two players who might start today, both of roughly equal merit with the bat. One has a handedness advantage, but is the worse fielder of the two. In that case, as long as his "over the course of a season" projection as a fielder at whatever position you want to slot him into is less than a 10-run drop from the guy he might replace, then he's a better option today.

We're not used to thinking of utility players as bat-first options, who would play below-average defense at three different infield positions. That guy might hook on as a 2B/3B/LF type (Howie Kendrick, come on down!) but teams usually think to themselves that they need as their utility infielder someone who "can handle" shortstop, the toughest of the infield spots to play. If someone can do that *and* hit well, he's probably already starting somewhere, so he's not available as a utility infielder. It's easier for those glove guys to find a job. In a world where the replacement for a shortstop *has to be* the designated utility infielder, that makes sense.

But as we talked about last week, we're living in a different world. The rate at which a replacement for a regular starter turns out to be *another starter* shifting over to cover has gone way up over the last five years. There was always some of it in the game, but this has been a supernova of switcheroos. Now if your second baseman is capable of playing a decent shortstop, that 2B/3B/LF guy can swap in. He's not actually playing shortstop, and maybe the defense suffers from the switch, but if he's got enough of a bat, he might outhit those extra fielding miscues. And in doing so, he is effectively your backup shortstop.

Somewhere along the lines, teams got hip to the idea of multi-positional play from their regulars. I've written before about how you can't just put a player, however athletic, into a new position and expect much at first. The data tell us that. Eventually, players can learn to be multi-positionalists, but it takes time, roughly on the order of two months, before they're OK. But there's a hidden message in there. If you give a player some reps at a new spot, he's a reasonably gifted athlete and somewhat smart and willing to learn, he could probably pick it up enough to get to "good enough," and it doesn't take forever. You just have to be purposeful about it. Maybe you get to the point where you can start to say "he's still below average but we could move him there and get another bat into the lineup, and it's a net win."

Teams have started to build those extra lessons into their player development program. It used to be seen as a mark of weakness to be relegated to "utility player" because that meant that you were a bench player (all those synonyms above come with a side of stigma). Now, it's a way of building a team. If you get a few reps in the minors (where it doesn't count) at a spot, you'll have at least played the spot at game speed before. There are limits to how far you can push that. A slow-footed "he's out in left field because we don't have the DH" guy is never going to play short, but maybe your third baseman can try second base and not look like a total moose out there.

⚾   ⚾   ⚾

Back to WAR. I'd argue that the world of starters and scrubs is slowly disintegrating, for good cause. In the event that a regular starter really does go down with an injury–ostensibly, the alternate universe scenario that WAR is attempting to model–it makes the team a little more resilient to replacing him. And the good news is that you're more likely to be able to replace him with the best of the bench bunch, rather than the third-best guy, because the best guy doesn't have to be an exact positional match for the guy who got hurt. And that's what the manager would want to do. He'd want to replace that long-term production, not with an amalgam of everyone else who played that position, but with the best guy available from his reserves.

Now this is still WAR. We still want to retain the principle that we should be measuring a player, and not his teammates. We need some sort of common baseline, and despite what I just said, we'll still need some sort of amalgam. To construct that, I give to you the idea of the tranche. The word, if you've not heard it before, refers to a piece of a whole that is somehow segmented off. It's often used in finance to talk about layers of a financial instrument.

Here, I want you to consider that there are 30 starters at each of the seven non-battery positions (catchers should have their own WAR, since only a catcher can replace a catcher). We can identify them by playing time, and we can futz around with the definition a little bit if we need to. Next, among those who aren't in that starting pool, we identify the top tranche of the 30 best bench players, which I would again identify by playing time, and then the second and third and fourth and so on. If a player were to disappear, his manager would probably want to take a guy from that top tranche of the bench to replace him. In a world where even the starters can slide around the field, that becomes more feasible.

We can take a look at that top tranche and say "How many of them showed that they are able to play (first, second, etc.)?" and therefore could have directly substituted for the starter? How many of them could have been a direct substitute for our injured player? We don't know whether one of them would be on *a specific* team, but we can say that 40 percent of the time, a manager would have been able to draw from tranche 1 in filling the role, and 35 percent from tranche 2. But on tranche 1, we can also look at how many of those players played a position that could have then shifted and covered for that spot. We'd need some eligibility criteria for all of this (probably a minimum number of games played) but it would just be a matter of multiplication. Shortstop would be harder to fill, and managers would probably be dipping a little further down in the talent pool, and so replacement level would be lower, as it is now.

Doing some quick analysis, I found that the difference in just batting linear weights (haven't even gotten into running or fielding) between tranche 1 and tranche 2 in 2019 was about 6.5 runs, prorated across 650 PA. Between tranche 1 and tranche 3, it's 10.8 runs. The ability to shift those plate appearances up the ladder has some real value.

This part is important. We can also give credit to starters for the positions that they showed an ability to play, even if they didn't play them (this is the guy fully capable of playing center, but who's in a corner because the team already has a good center fielder) because he allows a team to carry a player who hits like a left fielder to functionally be the team's backup center fielder. He facilitates that movement upward among the tranches. We can start to appreciate the difference between a left fielder who would never be able to hack it in center (and the compensatory move that his team would have to make) and the left fielder who could do it, but just didn't have to very often.

Past that, you can continue to use whatever hitting and fielding and running metrics you like to determine a player's value, but when we get down to constructing that baseline, I'd argue we need a better conceptual and mathematical framework. It's going to require some more #GoryMath than we're used to, but I'd argue it's a better conceptualization of the way that MLB actually plays the game in 2020. If...y'know...MLB plays in 2020. If WAR is going to be our flagship statistic among the *acronymati*, then we need to acknowledge that it contains some old and starting-to-be-out-of-date assumptions about the game. We may need to tinker with it. Here's my idea for how.

—*Russell A. Carleton is an author of Baseball Prospectus.*

Secondhand Sport

by Patrick Dubuque

Back before time stopped, I liked to go to thrift stores. Now that I'm older, I rarely ever buy anything—I don't need much in my life, now—but I still enjoy the old familiar circuit: check to see if there are baseball cards to write about, look for board or card games to play with the kids, scan for random ironic jerseys, hit the book section. It takes ten, maybe fifteen minutes. Thrift stores are the antithesis of modern online shopping, because you don't know what they have, and you don't even really know what you want. It's junk, literal junk, stuff other people thought was worthless. That's what makes it great.

In an idealized economy, thrift stores shouldn't exist. Everybody has a living wage, and every product has a durability that exactly matches its desired life; nothing should need to be given away, no one should need to be given to. But then, thrift stores shouldn't work on a customer experience level, either. You wouldn't think an ethos of "let's make everything disorganized and hard to find" would lead to customer satisfaction, but low-budget retailers like TJ Maxx and Ross thrive on this model. People like bargain hunting as much for the hunting as the bargain; it's part of the experience, spending time as if it's a wager. There's a thrill, occasionally, in inefficiency.

In sports, the modern overuse of the word "inefficiency" is a condemnation: It insinuates that there is *an* efficiency, a correct way to be found, and that all other ways are wrong ways. It's prevalent in baseball but hardly contained to it; the lifehack, the Silicon Valley disruption are other examples of productivity creep in our daily lives. Their modern success makes plenty of sense. Maximization of resources, after all, is its own puzzle, and an industry of European board games is founded upon it. It's fun to take a system and optimize it, unravel it like a sudoku puzzle. If there's only one kind of genius, after all, there's no way anyone can fail to appreciate it.

Baseball has been hacking away at these perceived inefficiencies since its inception: platoons, bullpens, farm systems were all installed to extract more out of the tools at hand. But it's been a particular badge of the sabermetric movement, from Ken Phelps and his All-Star Team to Ricardo Rincon and the darlings of *Moneyball*. It's business, but it's also an ethos: the idea that there's treasure among the trash, something we all failed to appreciate until someone brought it to light.

It's the myth that made Sidd Finch so enticing, that fuels so many "best shape" narratives and new pitch promises. We all, athletes and unathletic sportswriters, want to believe that there's genius trapped inside us, and that it's just a matter of puzzling out the combination to unlock it. That our art, our style is the next inefficiency, waiting for our own Billy Beane. It's why we root for underdogs, and why we're excited for the Mike Tauchmans and the Eurubiel Durazos, champions of skin-deep mediocrity.

Except we aren't anymore, really. The days of "Free X" have descended beyond the ring of irony and into obscurity. There are still Xs to be freed, or at least one X, duplicated endlessly: Mike Ford, Luke Voit, Max Muncy. The undervalued one-dimensional slugger demonstrated how the game hasn't quite culturally caught up to its logical extreme. But for those who don't fit the rather spacious mold, times are grimmer. As Rob Arthur revealed several months ago, there's been a marked increase in the number of sub-replacement relievers. It's the outcome of a greater number of teams forced to play out games without the talent to win them, but it's also emblematic of the modern tendency of teams to dispose of their disposable assets, burning through cost-controlled arms the way that man chopped down forests in *The Lorax*. Stuff just isn't built to outlive their original owners anymore.

It's unsurprising, given how well-mined the market for inefficiencies has been of late. The disciples of the early analytics departments, and the disciples of those, have proliferated the league, with only a few backwater holdouts. The league has grown smarter, but every team has learned the same lesson. In fact, the phenomenon creates a peculiar kind of feedback loop: As teams value a specific subset of players or skills, prospective athletes learn to increase their own marketability by conforming themselves to the demands of their prospective employers.

And that's tragic, in the way that the extinction of animals is tragic; a certain amount of biodiversity in baseball has been lost. Shortstops hit like outfielders. Pitchers don't hit at all. Only the catchers remain idiosyncratic, thanks to the defensive demands of their position; eventually they too will be required to produce like everyone else, or they'll meet the fate of their battery mates. A perfect economy requires perfect production.

I mentioned earlier that more and more, I leave thrift stores empty-handed. It is true that I am more discerning than in the past; my bookshelves are full, and there are more streaming films than I will ever be able to watch. But there are other factors at play.

Thrift stores are, in a way, the bond markets of retail. When the economy is rough and other retailers are struggling, more people look secondhand for their products. But as recently as last year, publications were noting a reversal of the trend: Companies like Goodwill and Savers were expanding despite a strong economy. Publications credited a heightened sense of environmentalism and a rejection of cutting-edge fashion as drivers behind the increase, though the more likely answer is the modern American economy hasn't showered its favors equally, particularly among the young.

But it is more than just the economy. Baseball and thrift stores share something else in common, evident in our current conversations about re-starting the sport: They live in the gray area between public service and private enterprise. Thrift stores provide affordable necessities to lower-class citizens, and collectibles and fashion for the middle-class. Because of the success of the latter, prices have gone up across the board. Especially in terms of clothing, the middle-class flight from fashion into vintage has instead carried the aftereffects of fashion, including its costs, into a territory where people just want clothes. But there's another factor in the rise of prices, in the form of the internet.

The Goodwills of the world have grown smarter, too, employing the internet to extract full value from their detritus. Ebay, similarly, has lost much of the charm it had as a new frontier around the turn of the century. Everything has a price point now; even individual taste is no match for the algorithm, because anything rare, no matter how niche its market, is a collectible to someone.

The internet has had the same effect on thrift stores that sabermetrics has had on baseball; its equivalent to OBP was the bar scanner. As detailed in Slate, the rise of second-party stores on eBay and Amazon birthed an entire industry of used-good salespeople, armed with PDAs and scanners, buying books for three dollars to sell online for five. The author, Michael Savitz, reports earning $60,000 by working nearly 80 hours a week; he makes it clear that this is not a vocation of his choosing. It's long hours, with no real creativity or individuality, skimming the cream off of a local establishment and flipping it to someone with a little more money on the other side of the country. And once the vocation exists, the obvious question arises: why wait to put the wares out on the shelves? Why allow value to exist at all?

Nothing is ruined. Thrift stores will continue to sell polo shirts and DVDs, and baseball will continue to exist and make or lose money, depending on who you believe. But as we continue to refine our knowledge, we lose something in the conquest for efficiency, a delight born out of the unknown. The problem isn't the efficiency itself; we can't blame the booksellers, or the people sweeping freeways to collect grams of platinum from damaged catalytic converters. The problem is a system that requires this sort of profit-skimming behavior in order to feed families (or, for corporations, maximize shareholder return).

In times like these, with the 2020 season on the brink and the collective bargaining agreement close behind, it can often feel like the current situation is untenable. It can't keep going like this, even if we don't know what to do about it. But as with thrift stores, there's an equally irresistible feeling that it *has* to keep going, that it would be unimaginable to not have this broken, amazing sport. Both industries exist on an invisible foundation of friction, of chaos and unpredictability, even as both see their foundations buffed down to a perfect, untouchable polish. But if COVID-19 and its financial ramifications do, as some have suggested, make it such that the baseball that returns is fundamentally different than the baseball that came before, perhaps this is the time to lean in, and change the game even more. Fix bunting. Make defense more difficult. Create viable, alternate strategies. Add some chaos back into baseball. It's fun when no one knows quite where things are.

—Patrick Dubuque is an author of Baseball Prospectus.

Steve Dalkowski Dreaming

by Steven Goldman

We dream of being a pitcher, of starring in the major leagues. Depending on your age and your sense of historical perspective, you might imagine yourself as Walter Johnson, throwing harder than anyone else—hitting more batters than anyone else, too, but always feeling bad about it. You could picture yourself as a Tom Seaver or a David Cone, with all the stuff in the world but still being cerebral about it, thinking about so much more than burning 'em in there. There are so many models one could choose: You could be a Lefty Gomez, Jim Bouton, or Bill Lee, skilled, but not taking the whole thing too seriously, or a Lefty Grove, Bob Gibson, or Steve Carlton, powerful but treating each start like a mission to be survived instead of a game to be enjoyed.

Very few would dream of being Steve Dalkowski, the former Baltimore Orioles prospect who died of COVID-19 last week at the age of 80. Yet, there is something just as noble in Dalkowski's negative accomplishments—and accomplishments is what they are—as there is in the precision-engineered pitching of a Greg Maddux. You have to be very good to be that bad. Dalkowski had all of the stuff of the greatest pitchers but none of the command; his story is not one of failing to conquer his limitations, but striving against one of the cruelest hands that fate or genetics or personality can deal us: A desire to achieve great things which is almost but not quite matched by the ability to meet that goal.

As with Johnson, Grove, Bob Feller, and the rest of the hard-throwing pitchers who played before the advent of modern radar guns, we have to take the word of the players and coaches who saw Dalkowski pitch as to his velocity. He was a hard-drinking, maximum-effort pitcher who, if their memories are to be believed, consistently threw over 100 miles per hour. His was the Maltese Fastball, the stuff that dreams are made of. The problem is that velocity without command and control is still a good distance from utility. Dalkowski was the most effective towel you could design for a fish, the sleekest bathing suit intended to be worn by an astronaut, but that doesn't mean he wasn't beautiful: We can appreciate a journey even if it doesn't end at the intended destination.

Whether because of sloppy mechanics he couldn't calm, an inability to understand that a consistent 98 in the strike zone would likely be more effective than a consistent 110 out of it, or all that beer, Dalkowski could never make the adjustments that pitchers like Feller and Nolan Ryan made before him, possibly because he had so far to go: Feller, who never pitched in the minors, came up at 17 and spent three years walking almost seven batters per nine innings before settling in at 3.8 beginning when he was 20. Ryan started out walking over six batters per nine but gradually improved as his long career played out; for him to go from 6.2 walks per nine with the 1966 Greenville Mets to 3.7 with the 1989 Texas Rangers represents a 40 percent reduction. An equivalent improvement by Dalkowski would still have left him walking over 11 batters per nine innings.

Dalkowski was like *The Room* of pitchers, a player so bad he became good again. Cal Ripken, Sr., who both played with and managed Dalkowski, recalled in a 1979 *Sporting News* "where are they now" piece the occasion when the pitcher crossed up his catcher and his fastball, "hit the plate umpire smack in the mask. The mask broke all to pieces and the umpire wound up in the hospital for three days with a concussion. If they ever had a radar gun in those days, I'll bet Dalkowski would have been timed at 110 miles an hour."

Signed by the Orioles out of New Britain High in Connecticut in 1957, Dalkowski was sent to Kingsport in the Appalachian League, where he pitched 62 innings. He allowed only 22 hits in 62 innings, or 3.2 per nine, a number with no equivalent in major league history (though Aroldis Chapman came close in 2014), and also struck out 121 (17.6 per nine) and walked 129 (18.7). He was also charged with 39 wild pitches. That June, one of his fastballs clipped a Dodgers prospect named Bob Beavers and carried away part of his ear. "The first pitch was over the backstop, the second pitch was called a strike, I didn't think it was," Beavers said last year. "The third pitch hit me and knocked me out, so I don't remember much after that. I couldn't get in the sun for a while, and I never did play baseball again." Former minor leaguer Ron Shelton based the *Bull Durham* pitcher Nuke LaLoosh on Dalkowski. And yet, to see him as a figure of fun, an amusing loser, is to misunderstand something unique and strange.

Dalkowski kept on posting some of the strangest lines in baseball history. Pitching for the Stockton Ports of the Class C California League in 1960, he struck out 262 and walked 262 in 170 innings. Yet, he did improve, especially after pitching for Earl Weaver at Elmira in 1962. Weaver had previously had Dalkowski at Aberdeen in 1959, but wasn't ready to grapple with him then. This time he was. "I had grown more and more concerned about players with great physical abilities who could not learn to correct certain basic deficiencies no matter how much you instructed or drilled them," he related in his autobiography, *It's What You Learn After You Know It All That Counts*. He got permission from the Orioles to give all of his players the Stanford-Binet IQ test. "Dalkowski finished in the 1 percentile in his ability to understand facts. Steve, it was said to say, had the ability to do everything but learn." [sic]

IQ tests are problematic diagnostic tools, so take Weaver's estimate of Dalkowski's mental capabilities with a grain of salt. What's important is that even if he got to the right answer by way of the wrong reason, Weaver had learned something valuable. His insight was to stop asking Dalkowski to learn new pitches and just let him get by with the two that he had. Were Dalkowski a prospect today, that would have been a no-brainer: Can't develop a third pitch? The bullpen is right over there, sir. Player development wasn't like that then, but Weaver, temporarily Dalkowski's mentor, could let him work with what he had. According to Weaver, the pitcher responded: "In the final 57 innings he pitched that season Dalkowski gave up 1 earned run, struck out 110 batters, and walked only 11." It's not true—as per the *Elmira Star-Gazette*, as of late July, Dalkowski had walked 71 in 106 innings and finished with 114 in 160 innings, which means Dalkowski's control actually faded at the end of the season rather than improved—but that doesn't mean it didn't happen in some sense, just that it didn't happen that way. Again, it's the journey, not the destination, and his ERA was 3.04 so *something* had gone right.

Also along the way: The next spring, Orioles manager Billy Hitchcock was rooting for Dalkowski to make the team as a long-man—maybe Weaver had gotten through to him. There were things out of Weaver's control, like the universe's twisted sense of humor: that March, Dalkowski's elbow went "twang."

You sometimes read that it was the Orioles' insistence on Dalkowski learning the curve that did him in, but even if they hadn't learned their lesson, the injury was probably just a coincidence: Dalkowski had thrown an incredible number of pitches over the previous few years. Still, it testifies to the dangers of trying to get what you want and risking the loss of what you had. Dalkowski tried to come back, but the 110-mph stuff was gone. A pitcher with no control and no stuff is…a civilian. What followed were years of vagabond living, arrests for drunkenness. There were Alcoholics Anonymous meetings, assistance from baseball alumni associations, but none of it took. From the 1990s until the time of his passing he dwelt in an assisted living facility, suffering from alcohol-related dementia. He'd been a heavy drinker since his teenage years. As with all those pitches per game, there was a price to be paid. You make choices on the journey and some of them are irrevocable. It's like a fairy tale: "Bite of poison apple? Don't mind if I do."

In the aforementioned *Sporting News* profile, Chuck Stevens, the head of the Association of Professional Ballplayers of America, a ballplayer charity, said, "I've got nothing against drinking. I do it myself sometimes. But, I don't condone common drunkenness. We went through lots of heartache and many dollars, but Dalkowski didn't want to help himself and we weren't going to keep him drunk." The journey is *un*like a fairy tale: No one will come along and kiss it better, not if they're busy forming judgments.

In the end, we are left with a sort of philosophical chicken/egg conundrum: Is failing to meet your goals evidence of unfulfilled potential or the lack of it? Isn't what you did by definition what you were capable of doing? Or could you have broken through to something better with the right help, the right lucky break? These are unanswerable questions, and how we try to answer them may say more about us than about the people we're judging.

No pitcher ever has it easy. *All* pitchers must work hard. *All* pitchers must refine their craft. It's almost never just about *stuff*. Dalkowski dreaming is no insult to the great pitchers who made it; from Pete Alexander to Max Scherzer, they have all earned their way up. And yet, if it is true that we can only do as much as we can do, then the journey would be more of an adventure, the ultimate triumph or defeat more noble, if like Dalkowski we lacked 100 percent of the confidence, the command, the self-possession, the commitment, the resistance to making bad decisions that so many great players possess—to be gloriously human. Or, to put it more succinctly, it would be fun to be able to throw as hard as any person ever has. Even if just for a moment, and even if nothing more came of it than that, no one could say you hadn't lived life to the fullest.

—*Steven Goldman is an author of Baseball Prospectus.*

A Reward For A Functioning Society

by Cory Frontin and Craig Goldstein

On July 5, Nationals reliever Sean Doolittle said in the middle of a press conference regarding the restart of Major League Baseball and what would later be known as summer camp, "sports are like the reward of a functioning society." This sentence was amidst a much longer, thoughtful reply about the societal and health conditions under which MLB players were being brought back. It's a very similar sentiment to one Jane McManus used on April 7, when she discussed the White House's meeting with sports commissioners. She said "sports are the effect of a functioning society—not the precursor."

Both versions of the same sentiment spoke to a laudable ideal in the context of a country that was not addressing a rampaging virus, and opting instead to bring sports back for the feeling of normalcy rather than the reality of it. "Priorities," as McManus said.

On Wednesday, the NBA's Milwaukee Bucks conducted a wildcat/political strike, refusing to come out for Game 5 of their playoff series against the Orlando Magic. The Magic refused to accept the forfeit, and shortly thereafter other playoff series were threatened by player strikes. Eventually the league moved to postpone that day's games, folding to players leveraging their united power.

The backdrop against which these actions took place was the shooting by police of Jacob Blake. Blake was shot in the back seven times by police, as he attempted to get into his vehicle. He managed to survive the assault, but is paralyzed from the waist down.

⚾   ⚾   ⚾

The step taken to walk out, first by the Milwaukee Bucks, then subsequently by other NBA, WNBA, and MLB teams, was a step toward upholding the virtue of the sentiment described by McManus and Doolittle. But that sentiment does not align with the broad history of sports in this and other countries, a history that contradicts the core of the idealistic statement.

Sports have been a significant part of American society for most of its existence, expanding in importance and influence in recent years. The idea that society was functioning in a way that was worthy of the reward of sports for most of that time is laughable. Much of America is not functioning and has not functioned for Black people, full stop. The oppressed people at the center of this political act by players, specifically Black players, in concert throughout the NBA and in fits and starts throughout Major League Baseball, have not known a society that functions for them rather than *because* of them.

Politics has been part of the sports landscape since the inception of sport, but for just about as long people have bemoaned its presence. Sports are to be an escape, it is said. An escape from what, though? A functioning society?

No, the presence of sports has never signified a cultural or political system that is on the up and up. Rather, the presence of sports *reflect and reinforce the society* that produces them.

⚾   ⚾   ⚾

The Negro Leagues were born out of societal dysfunction. The need for entirely separate leagues, composed of Black and Latino players barred from the Major Leagues because of racism? That is not a functioning society, and yet there were sports.

Even the integration of players from the Negro Leagues resulted in a transfer of power and wealth from Black-owned businesses and communities and into white ones, mirroring the dysfunction that had bled into every aspect of American society at the time. Japheth Knopp noted in the Spring 2016 Baseball Research Journal:

> The manner in which integration in baseball—and in American businesses generally—occurred was not the only model which was possible. It was likely not even the best approach available, but rather served the needs of those in already privileged positions who were able to control not only the manner in which desegregation occurred, but the public perception of it as well in order to exploit the situation for financial gain. Indeed, the very word integration may not be the most applicable in this context because what actually transpired was not so much the fair and equitable combination of two subcultures into one equal and more homogenous group, but rather the reluctant allowance—under certain preconditions—for African Americans to be assimilated into white society.

To understand the value of a movement, though, is not to understand how it is co-opted by ownership, but to know the people it brings together and what they demand. When Jackie Robinson—the player who demarcated the inevitability of the end of the Negro leagues—attended the March on Washington for Jobs and Freedom in 1963, he did so with his family and marched alongside the people. He stood alongside hundreds of thousands to fight for their common civil and labor rights. "The moral arc of the universe is long," many freedom fighters have echoed, "but it bends towards justice." The bend, it is less frequently said, happens when a great mass of people place the moral arc of the universe on their knee and apply force, as Jackie, his family, and thousands of others did that day.

⚾   ⚾   ⚾

Of course, taking the moral arc of the universe down from the mantle and bending it is not without risk. Perhaps the outsized influence of athletes is itself a mark of a dysfunctional society, but, nonetheless, hundreds of athletes woke up on Wednesday morning with the power to bring in millions of dollars in revenues. That very power, as we would come to find out, was matched with the equal and opposite power to *not* bring those revenues. That power, in hands ranging from the Milwaukee Bucks, to Kenny Smith in the *Inside the NBA* Studio, from the unexpected ally, Josh Hader, and his largely white teammates to the notably Black Seattle Mariners, would be exercised for a single demand: the end to state violence against Black people. Not unlike the March itself, it sat at the intersection of the civil rights of Black Americans and bold labor action. The March on Washington stood in the face of a false notion of integration—against an integration of extraction but not one of equality—and proposed something different. Just the same, the acts of solidarity of August 26, 2020 will be remembered in stark defiance of MLB's BLM-branded, but ultimately empty displays on opening weekend.

Bold defiance like this can never be without risk. By choosing to exercise this power, the Milwaukee Bucks took a risk. They risked vitriol and backlash from those they disagreed with. They risked fines or seeing their contracts voided, as a walkout like this is prohibited by their CBA. They risked forfeiting a playoff game, one that, as the No. 1 seed in the playoffs, they'd worked all year to attain. They didn't know how Orlando would respond. It wasn't clear that other teams throughout the league would follow suit in solidarity. And it wasn't known the league would accept these actions and moderately co-opt them by "postponing" games that would have featured no players.

If the league reschedules the games, some of the athletes' risk—their shared sacrifice—will be diminished, in retrospect. But they did not know any of that when they took that risk. And it is often left to athletes to take these risks when others in society won't, especially those of their same socioeconomic status and levels of influence.

It is athletes, specifically BIPOC athletes, that take them, though, because they live with the risk of being something other than white in this country every day. They are no strangers to the realities of police brutality. It seems incongruous then, to say that sports are a reward for a functioning society when we rely on athletes to lead us closer to being a functioning society. Luckily, our beloved athletes, WNBA players first and foremost among them, understand what sports truly are: a pipebender for the moral arc of the universe.

—Craig Goldstein is editor in chief of Baseball Prospectus. Cory Frontin is an author of Baseball Prospectus.

Index of Names

Alford, Anthony 68

Bashlor, Tyler 77

Bednar, David 78

Bolton, Cody 96

Brault, Steven 42

Brubaker, JT 44

Castro, Rodolfo 99

Cederlind, Blake 79, 98

Craig, Will 69

Crick, Kyle 80

Crowe, Wil 81, 98

Cruz, Oneil 70

Difo, Wilmer 71

Evans, Phillip 16

Feliz, Michael 82

Fraizer, Matthew 99

Frazier, Adam 18

Fulmer, Carson 46

Gonzales, Nick 71, 92

González, Erik 20

Goodwin, Brian 22

Hartlieb, Geoff 48

Hayes, Ke'Bryan 24, 91

Holland, Derek 50

Howard, Sam 52

Jones, Jared 83, 98

Kela, Keone 83

Keller, Mitch 54

Kranick, Max 97

Kuhl, Chad 56

Loree, Mike 84

Malone, Brennan 85, 94

Martin, Mason 72, 99

Mitchell, Cal 96

Mlodzinski, Carmen 85, 98

Moran, Colin 26

Murphy, John Ryan 72

Neverauskas, Dovydas 58

Newman, Kevin 28

Oliva, Jared 74

Osuna, José 30

Peguero, Liover 75, 93

Perez, Michael 32

Polanco, Gregory 34

Ponce, Cody 60

Priester, Quinn 86, 93

Reynolds, Bryan 36

Rodríguez, Richard 62

Shreve, Chasen 64

Soriano, Jose 87, 99

Stallings, Jacob 38

Stratton, Chris 66

Swaggerty, Travis 76, 95

Thomas, Tahnaj 94

Tucker, Cole 40

Wang, Wei-Chung 87

Wolters, Tony 76

Yajure, Miguel 88

Yang, Yao-Hsun 89

Yean, Eddy 99

For the Joy of Keeping Score

THIRTY81 Project is an ongoing graphic design project focused on the ballparks of baseball. Since being established in 2013, scorecards have been a fundemantal part of the effort. Each two-page card is uniquely ballpark-centric — there are 30 variants — and designed with both beginning and veteran scorekeepers in mind. Evolving over the years with suggestions from fans, broadcasters, and official scorers, the sheets are freely available to everyone as printable letter-size PDFs at the project webshop: www.THIRTY81Project.com

Download, Print, Score, Repeat ...

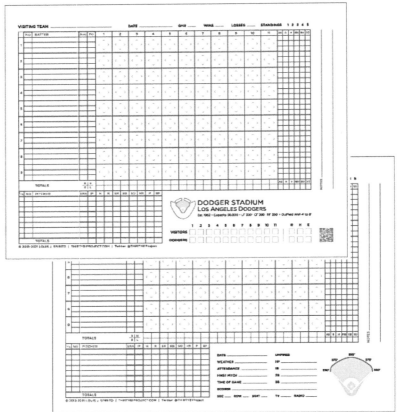

Scorecard design ©2013-2021 Louis J. Spirito | THIRTY81Project